# chocolate

# chocolate

Linda Collister

photography by Martin Brigdale

RYLAND
PETERS
& SMALL
LONDON  NEW YORK

Dedicated to Emily, Daniel and Stevie, with love.

First published in Great Britain in 2002
by Ryland Peters & Small
Kirkman House,
12–14 Whitfield Street
London W1T 2RP
www.rylandpeters.com

10 9 8 7 6 5 4 3 2 1

Text © Linda Collister 2002
Design and photographs
© Ryland Peters & Small 2002

Printed in China

ISBN 1 84172 320 7

A CIP record for this book is available
from the British Library.

**Senior Designer** Steve Painter
**Commissioning Editor** Elsa Petersen-Schepelern
**Editor** Kathy Steer
**Production** Meryl Silbert
**Art Director** Gabriella Le Grazie
**Publishing Director** Alison Starling

**Food Stylists** Bridget Sargeson, Linda Collister
**Stylist** Helen Trent
**Indexer** Hilary Bird

**Author's acknowledgements**
I would like to thank the following for their help with this book:
Elsa Petersen-Schepelern, Steve Painter, Martin Brigdale, Helen Trent,
Barbara Levy, Bridget Sargeson, Annette and Will Hertz. Thanks also to
Michelle Kershaw and Lakeland Limited for baking equipment, Alan and
Simon Silverwood of Alan Silverwood Ltd for loaf tins and baking sheets and
Pam Bewley for the Magimix food processor. Robin Kendal, Michael Levy,
Jean-Jacques Bernachon, Sara Jayne Staines and Chantal Coady helped
me with my chocolate education (though any mistakes are mine.) And last
but certainly not least Alan Hertz.

**Notes**

All spoon measurements are level unless otherwise specified.

All eggs are medium, unless otherwise specified. Uncooked or partly cooked
eggs should not be served to the very young, the very old, those with
compromised immune systems, or to pregnant women.

Before baking, weigh or measure all ingredients exactly and prepare baking
tins or sheets.

Ovens should be preheated to the specified temperature. Recipes in this
book were tested in 4 different kinds of ovens – all work slightly differently.
I recommend using an oven thermometer and consulting the maker's
handbook for special instructions.

# contents

# the food of the gods ...

For most of its long history, chocolate was a luxury, reserved for privileged people and special occasions. But *Theobroma cacao* – the 'food of the gods' – was first appreciated not just for its taste, but for its economic, spiritual and medicinal virtues.

Wild cacao is native to the lowland jungles of Mexico and Central America, and the ancient Maya people who lived there turned the bitter, inedible seeds of cacao into foamy beverages used in religious rituals. In the Aztec empire, the male elite also used the drink called *xocolatl* (bitter water) in their daily religious rituals, as well as an aphrodisiac and a health tonic.

Although when Columbus 'discovered' the New World, he saw cocoa beans, he never tasted them. It was the Spanish conquistador, Cortés, who saw cocoa beans used as currency by the Aztecs and realized their economic value. He introduced the drink to the Spanish court as a medicine, and founded plantations in the new Spanish territories.

For the first hundred years or so, its use was confined to the court, nobility and the Church, but with royal intermarriage, the fashion for chocolate drinks spread throughout Europe. By the time of the restoration of King Charles II in 1660, the English thought of chocolate as a stimulant and medicine, a cure for hangovers and a source of strength and energy. Then, by the early 18th century, Dr Hans Sloane thought of adding milk and using it as a palatable drink for Queen Anne's sickly children. He sold the recipe to the Quakers, who saw it as a healthy alternative to alcohol.

Although cocoa was once used exclusively to make beverages, we now more often associate chocolate with a solid bar of confectionery. The maker uses a mixture of dried beans and the flavour of the finished chocolate depends largely on the quality of the beans and the skill of the blender. The king of chocolatiers, Jean-Jacques Bernachon in Lyon, France, uses up to twelve varieties and compares the beans to the *premier crus* wines of Bordeaux.

The flavour of chocolate is also determined by the way the dried beans are roasted, as it is very easy to scorch them. After roasting, the 'nibs' are gently crushed to make a paste of minuscule particles. The resulting paste is blended with additional melted cocoa butter, real vanilla and a little sugar. This mixture is slowly melted and stirred to release the flavours and to give the smoothest possible texture.

The percentage of cocoa solids in the chocolate should be on the label of your chocolate bar. About 60–70 per cent is perfect, but a high percentage is not a guarantee of good flavour – the chocolate must be perfectly balanced. It shouldn't leave your mouth feeling greasy or astringent, nor should it have a harsh or burnt aftertaste. It's worthwhile trying several different brands.

Using the best ingredients will make a difference to the taste and quality of any recipe you make. Choose the finest chocolate you can afford and look out for organic and fairtrade brands.

Today, chocolate is an enduring passion for millions of people. It is now known to contain phosphorous, iron, calcium and theobromine, which affects the central nervous system and acts as an antidepressant. I've heard it said that women feel for chocolate the way men feel for football. I hope you'll love these recipes as much as I do.

# techniques

The techniques shown here are demonstrated by Robin Kendal, Chocolatier-in-Chief at the legendary English tea rooms, Bettys of Harrogate in Yorkshire. He has been making chocolates by hand at Bettys for 25 years (they get through 8 tonnes of Belgian chocolate each year). He now also demonstrates and teaches chocolate work at their newly built cooking school near Harrogate.

# melting chocolate

**1** To chop chocolate, use a large sharp knife and a clean dry board (make sure the board doesn't have any lingering odours from chopping garlic or onions).

Put the evenly chopped chocolate into a dry heatproof bowl and set over a saucepan of steaming but not boiling water. The water should not touch the base of the bowl or start to boil.

**2** As the chocolate starts to melt, stir gently with a spatula or wooden spoon, so the chocolate will melt evenly rather than in hot spots.

**3** When the chocolate has become completely smooth, remove the bowl from the heat to avoid overheating.

**Note** If the chocolate becomes too warm or comes into contact with a drop of water or steam, it will become stiff and hard rather than smooth and liquid. This is called 'seizing' and means that the chocolate is unusable and cannot be saved.

# tempering*

**1** To temper chocolate, melt it as shown on page 11, then raise the temperature of the steaming water so the chocolate temperature reaches 45–48°C (113–118°F). Stir gently with a spatula, so the chocolate heats evenly. Remove the bowl from the heat as soon as it reaches 45°C (113°F), because the chocolate will start to seize if it reaches 50°C (122°F). In addition, it may not set to the desired finish and may also develop a bloom (see note opposite).

*Note Tempering means to melt and cool chocolate to make it shiny, smooth and even in colour. In this form, it may be used in many recipes as an icing or decoration, or in making chocolates.

**2** Next, the temperature has to be reduced to 27°C (80°F). This can be done in two ways.

Firstly, by adding chopped chocolate to the bowl. Add about one-quarter of the initial weight of chocolate used, then stir gently with a spatula, so the chocolate melts and lowers the temperature of the chocolate in the bowl to 27°C (80°F).

**Alternatively**, when the chocolate has reached 45°C (113°F), put the bowl into a larger bowl filled with cool, not cold, water and stir gently with a spatula until the temperature is 27°C (80°F). Make sure that no water comes into contact with the chocolate.

**3** When ready to use, reheat the chocolate to 29–30°C (84–86°F) by setting the bowl over a saucepan of gently steaming water (do not let the base of the bowl touch the water). Stir gently with a spatula and use as soon as the chocolate reaches the correct temperature.

**4** To test if the chocolate has been correctly tempered, dip the tip of a clean dry palette knife into the chocolate, then cool and let set. When properly tempered, the chocolate on the upper surface will appear smooth and evenly coloured rather than streaky or slightly textured. Peel the chocolate away from the knife – the underside should be shiny.

**Note** The larger the quantity of chocolate, the easier it is to control temperatures – about 250 g is easy to handle. Any excess can be reset and stored for future use. Pour the excess into ice cube trays, let set, then press out and store in a plastic container.

**Bloom** If the chocolate is stored incorrectly, either at a very high temperature or exposed to a wide range of temperatures, the cocoa butter starts to crystallize on the surface as dull grey streaks. This is called a 'bloom'. (It does not affect the flavour.)

# dipping and coating

**Above** To give a smooth, professional finish to a handmade chocolate, drop it into a bowl of tempered chocolate (page 12). Lift it out using a round wire tool (left) or chocolatier's fork (right), available through Mail Order Sources and Websites (page 126). Bounce the fork up and down several times on the surface of the melted chocolate so the surface tension pulls off the excess chocolate. Use the round wire tool for round chocolates and the chocolatier's fork for any other shape with a flat base.

Put the dipped chocolates onto a baking sheet lined with non-stick baking parchment or greaseproof paper and let set.

**Above** To give a twirled top to round chocolates (left), press the round wire tool gently onto the surface of the chocolate, then lift and twirl. To give a ridged top to square shapes (right), drag the prongs of the fork across the surface of the chocolate to leave a striped mark.

Let set. Store in an airtight container in a cool place or in the refrigerator.

# making chocolate curls

Chocolate curls and shavings give a professional finish to a cake or pudding.

1  Make tempered chocolate as shown on pages 12–13, then pour the chocolate onto a clean marble slab (this will help to cool the chocolate very quickly).

2  Quickly, before the chocolate sets, use a spatula to spread the chocolate thinly to about 2–3 mm thick.

3  Keep working the chocolate with the spatula, until it sets and becomes matt and dull rather than shiny.

4  To make the curls, hold a large sharp knife at an angle away from you and shave the top off the sheet of chocolate, pushing the knife through the chocolate and ending at the far edge. Store in an airtight container in a cool place.

**Note**  The edges may be too thick to make good curls, but keep them and any unsatisfactory attempts – you can melt and reuse them.

# making solid moulded chocolates

**1** Make tempered chocolate as shown on pages 12–13. Use a ladle to overfill the chocolate moulds with the chocolate – the moulds should be clean, but do not oil or grease them.

**2** Gently tap the moulds on the work surface to expel any air bubbles.

**3** Scrape off the excess chocolate with a palette knife to give a completely flat surface. The chocolate contracts as it sets, so it's important to cool the chocolate quickly. Cover with clingfilm to avoid any condensation, then refrigerate, ideally at 11°C (51°F). It will take about 20 minutes to set.

**4** To remove, invert the mould over a sheet of non-stick baking parchment or greaseproof paper and tap gently to loosen the chocolate. Store in an airtight container in a cool place.

# making hollow moulded chocolate shapes

**1** Make tempered chocolate as shown on pages 12–13. Use a ladle to pour the chocolate into the clean, unoiled mould.

**2** Swirl the mould so the chocolate completely coats the inside of the mould.

**3** Pour out the extra chocolate, then scrape the excess from the rim of the mould with a palette knife. Set the mould upside down on a baking sheet lined with non-stick baking parchment or greaseproof paper and give a gentle tap to expel any air bubbles. Put in the refrigerator and let set for about 20 minutes. Give the mould a second coat of chocolate in the same way as before, then chill until set.

**4** When set, lift off the plastic mould. To join two halves of the egg, put the halves back into their moulds (try not to touch the tops or the shiny surfaces will look fingered) and, using a piping bag or knife, pipe or spread a little melted chocolate onto the rim. Press the two halves together and let set in the refrigerator for about 20 minutes before unmoulding again. Store in an airtight container in a cool place.

# making stippled easter eggs

To make a two- or three-tone egg, use tempered chocolate in
at least two different colours – milk, white or plain.

**Above** Finger-painted Easter
egg (front) and Stippled Easter
Egg (rear).

**1** Make tempered chocolate
as shown on pages 12–13.
Use two types of chocolate
such as plain and white.
Holding the mould by the rim,
use a clean dry sponge to dab
the thinnest possible coat of
the first colour chocolate into
the mould, then put into the
refrigerator and let set for
about 20 minutes.

**2** Using a ladle, pour in
tempered chocolate of a
contrasting colour.

**3** Swirl the chocolate, pour out
the excess, then put the mould
into the refrigerator and let set
for about 20 minutes. Give the
mould a second coat of the
solid colour and let set in the
refrigerator.

# making finger-painted easter eggs

**1** Finger-painting with chocolate gives an abstract finish. Dip your finger into melted tempered chocolate and paint the mould in a speckled design. Put into the refrigerator and let set for about 20 minutes.

**2** Repeat, filling in some of the gaps with another colour chocolate. Put into the refrigerator and let set for about 20 minutes.

**3** Fill the mould with a third colour, swirl and tip out the excess chocolate.

**4** Put the mould into the refrigerator and let set for about 20 minutes, then add a second coat of the same colour and let set. The eggs can be joined together with melted chocolate (see page 17).

# chocolates

Hand-made chocolates are the best of indulgences – just one perfect chocolate can make anyone feel special, and a box of hand-mades will make a terrific gift. Each brand of chocolate has slightly different characteristics – try out several to find the one you prefer. Store the finished chocolates in an airtight plastic container in the refrigerator and eat at room temperature.

# chocolate dials

150 g plain chocolate
1 recipe praline (page 30)
50 g large seedless raisins

*a baking sheet lined with
non-stick baking parchment*

Makes about 20

Perfect to serve with after-dinner coffee, these chocolate discs are decorated with raisins and chunks of praline.

Put the chocolate into a heatproof bowl set over a saucepan of steaming but not boiling water and melt gently (do not let the base of the bowl touch the water). Let cool for 2 minutes. Drop 1 teaspoon of the chocolate onto a baking sheet lined with non-stick baking parchment, then spread it to a disc, about 4 cm diameter. Press 2 hazelnut-sized pieces of praline and 2 large seedless raisins into the chocolate. Repeat using the remaining chocolate, praline and raisins. Leave to set in a cool place or the refrigerator, then peel off the paper. Store in an airtight container. Best eaten within 1 week.

# chocolate salami

150 g plain chocolate
100 ml double cream
½ recipe praline (page 30)
50 g crystallized fruit, finely chopped

*non-stick baking parchment*

Makes about 20

A mixture of chocolate, praline and crystallized fruits is shaped into a sausage, then thinly sliced to resemble a salami – popular in Italy around Christmas.

Put the chocolate into a bowl. Put the cream into a saucepan, heat until hot, then pour over the chocolate. Stir the praline and crystallized fruit into the chocolate mixture. Spoon onto a sheet of non-stick baking parchment, then shape into a sausage, about 4 cm thick. Wrap up in the paper and chill until firm. Remove the paper, cut into thin slices and serve.

# ginger chocolates

60 g plain chocolate, melted
60 g crystallized ginger (about 20 pieces)

*bamboo skewers*

*a baking sheet lined with
non-stick baking parchment*

Makes about 20

My editor has a will of iron – she can pass by a box of chocolates without a qualm – but offer her a ginger chocolate and she becomes as incoherent as most chocoholics.

Melt the chocolate as described on page 11. Spear each piece of ginger with a bamboo skewer, then dip the ginger halfway into the chocolate. Alternatively, follow the method in Step 1, page 14 to cover the ginger completely.

# tiny florentines

At holiday time, look out for crystallized fruits to replace sultanas in the mixture. When cold, the flat side of each Florentine is coated with plain or white chocolate, then combed to give a wavy pattern or feathered (dragged) design.

85 g unsalted butter

85 g golden syrup

30 g plain flour

60 g chopped almonds

30 g chopped mixed peel

60 g sultanas or crystallized fruits

60 g glacé cherries, chopped

110 g chocolate – plain or white – or some of each, melted

*2 baking sheets lined with non-stick baking parchment*

Makes about 20

Put the butter and golden syrup into a medium, heavy-based saucepan and heat until melted. Stir in all the remaining ingredients except the chocolate.

Put teaspoons of the mixture onto the prepared baking sheets, spacing them well apart. Flatten lightly, then bake in a preheated oven at 180°C (350°F) Gas 4 for 7–8 minutes until light golden brown. Remove from the oven and let cool for 1–2 minutes or until firm enough to transfer to a wire rack to cool completely.

When cool, coat the flat underside of each Florentine with melted chocolate and, using a serrated icing spatula or fork, make a wavy pattern in the chocolate. Leave to set, chocolate side up. Store in a cool place in an airtight container.

Best eaten within 1 week.

# chocolate truffles

This basic recipe is sublime, but you can also add liqueur to the mixture.

200 ml double cream

300 g plain chocolate, finely chopped

To coat

250 g plain or white chocolate, melted

50 g finest quality cocoa powder, sifted

*a piping bag fitted with a 1 cm plain nozzle (optional)*

*several baking sheets lined with non-stick baking parchment or wax paper*

Makes 50

**1** Put the cream into a saucepan and heat gently until boiling. Remove from the heat and let cool for several minutes.

Put the chopped chocolate into a heatproof bowl, then pour over the hot cream\*. Set aside for a couple of minutes.

**\*Note** If you wish to add alcohol, do so before adding the cream. Suitable choices include 3 tablespoons Drambuie, dark rum, Cognac, Tia Maria or orange liqueur.

**2** Stir gently until just smooth – do not over-mix at this stage. Let cool.

When the mixture is cold but not set, beat vigorously with a wooden spoon until very thick and much lighter in colour and texture.

**3** Spoon the mixture into a piping bag fitted with a 1 cm plain nozzle.

**4** Pipe marble-sized pieces of the mixture onto the prepared baking sheets. Chill until very firm.

**Alternatively**, you can also use a teaspoon, or roll the mixture into balls with your hands. Chill until very firm.

**5** When you are ready to finish the truffles, put the 250 g chopped chocolate into a dry heatproof bowl and set over a saucepan of steaming but not boiling water. The water should not touch the base of the bowl or start to boil (page 11). If you like, the chocolate may also be tempered (page 12).

Remove the bowl from the heat.

**6** Using 2 forks, briefly dip each truffle into the chocolate until coated.

Return the coated truffles to the lined sheets and leave until the coating chocolate is almost set (if the truffles are very cold, this will be immediate).

**7** While the coating chocolate is still soft, roll the truffles in cocoa powder. Store in an airtight container in a cool place or the refrigerator until ready to serve.

These eggs made of chocolate and praline (a crunchy mixture of brittle caramel and toasted nuts) can be found in good chocolate shops in France and Italy around Easter. After the filled eggs have set, the shells can be decorated using edible colours, then arranged in an egg box or basket.

# surprise eggs

6 very fresh eggs, with pretty shells

150 g plain chocolate, finely chopped

100 ml double cream

Praline*

50 g whole unblanched almonds

50 g whole skinned hazelnuts

100 g caster sugar

a baking sheet, well-oiled

Makes 6

Using the tip of a small, sharp knife, gently cut a small hole in the pointed end of each egg, then carefully snip away the shell with scissors to cut off the top, leaving a hole about 2 cm across. Empty out the eggs by shaking them over a bowl – the contents can be saved for omelettes or scrambled eggs. Wash the empty shells thoroughly, then set them on a piece of greaseproof paper in a baking dish and dry them in a preheated oven at 150°C (300°F) Gas 2 for about 15 minutes. Let cool.

Meanwhile, to make the praline, put the nuts and sugar into a small, heavy-based saucepan and heat gently on top of the stove. Stir frequently with a wooden spoon until the sugar melts, then watch it carefully, stirring frequently, as it cooks and turns chestnut brown and the nuts start to pop. Take care with hot caramel, because splashes can burn you.

Lift the saucepan off the heat, quickly pour the mixture onto the oiled baking sheet and, using a wooden spoon, spread it out evenly. Leave until completely cold and set, then coarsely break up the praline with a rolling pin or grind it in a food processor.

Put the chopped chocolate into a heatproof bowl. Put the cream into a heavy-based saucepan, heat until hot but not boiling, then pour it over the chocolate. Leave for 1 minute, then stir gently. Let cool for 5–10 minutes until thick, then stir in the praline. Stand the egg shells upright in an egg box or rack and carefully spoon the chocolate mixture into the shells. Chill overnight until firm, then remove from the refrigerator 2 hours before serving.

*Note Use this praline recipe to make the Chocolate Dials and Chocolate Salami on page 23.

# baking

No scent has ever been invented that rivals the aroma of chocolate baking. It fills the whole house so everyone knows just what lies in store for them. Here's a fabulous array of cakes, biscuits, muffins, brownies, even doughnuts – from fast and simple to simply luxurious.

A favourite with many generations of cake-lovers, this simple creamed sponge is the basis of scores of recipes, from fairy cakes to richly iced gâteaux and hot puddings. For the best results, use large eggs and unsalted butter, all at room temperature. An electric mixer is a good investment if you like making cakes – it gives the mixture a much lighter texture, as well as saving time and arm power. The sponges can be sandwiched and topped with a variety of fillings and icings (pages 38–39), such as the ganache shown here, or with whipped cream or dark cherry jam.

# classic chocolate sponge cake

175 g unsalted butter, at room temperature

175 g caster sugar

3 large eggs, at room temperature

1 teaspoon vanilla essence

150 g self-raising flour

30 g cocoa powder

2 tablespoons milk

2 sandwich tins, 20 cm diameter, buttered and base-lined

Serves 8

Put the butter into a mixing bowl and, using a wooden spoon or electric mixer, beat until creamy. Beat in the sugar and continue beating until the mixture is very light and fluffy.

Break the eggs into a jug or bowl, add the vanilla essence and beat with a fork until slightly frothy. Gradually beat the eggs into the butter and sugar mixture, beating well after each addition. Sift the flour and cocoa onto the mixture, add the milk, then, using a large metal spoon, gently fold into the creamed mixture. As soon as the mixture is thoroughly blended, with no visible streaks, divide it equally between the 2 prepared tins and spread evenly.

Bake in a preheated oven at 180°C (350°F) Gas 4 for 15–20 minutes or until the sponge springs back when gently pressed in the centre, is starting to colour on top and has shrunk away from the sides of the tin. Turn out onto a wire rack, remove the lining paper and let cool completely before filling and icing.

Store in an airtight container in a cool place. Best eaten within 48 hours.

# classic chocolate sponge cake variations

## cupcakes

175 ml full-cream milk

60 g plain chocolate, finely chopped

125 g caster sugar

60 g unsalted butter, at room temperature

1/2 teaspoon vanilla essence

1 large egg, beaten

150 g self-raising flour

2 tablespoons chocolate chips or chopped plain chocolate

fudge topping (page 39), (optional)

*a 12-hole muffin or deep bun tray, lined with paper cases*

Makes 12

Put the milk into a saucepan and heat until just scalding. Put the chocolate and one-third of the sugar into a bowl, pour over the milk and stir until smooth. Let cool. Put the butter into a bowl, then add the remaining sugar and vanilla. Using a wooden spoon, beat until light and fluffy, then gradually beat in the egg. Stir in the chocolate mixture alternately with the flour. Stir in the chips. Spoon into paper cases until three-quarters full. Bake in a preheated oven at 180°C (350°F) Gas 4 for 15–18 minutes until the cakes spring back when pressed in the centre. Let cool, then add fudge topping, if using.

## fairy cakes

175 g unsalted butter, at room temperature

175 g caster sugar

3 large eggs, at room temperature

1 teaspoon vanilla essence

150 g self-raising flour

30 g cocoa powder

2 tablespoons milk

chocolate toppings (pages 38–39), (optional)

*several mince pie, bun or muffin tins, lined with paper cases*

Makes 24

Put all the ingredients into a mixing bowl and, using a wooden spoon or electric mixer, mix until thoroughly blended – if using an electric mixer, use medium speed. Spoon about 1 tablespoon of the mixture into each paper case, until half full. Bake in a preheated oven at 180°C (350°F) Gas 4 for 12–15 minutes until the sponge springs back when gently pressed in the centre. Let cool on a wire rack. Serve plain or spread with a chocolate topping of your choice.

## gâteau arabica

225 g unsalted butter, at room temperature

300 g light muscovado sugar

4 large eggs, beaten

100 g plain flour

125 g cocoa powder

2 teaspoons baking powder

4 tablespoons espresso coffee or 4 teaspoons instant coffee dissolved in 4 tablespoons hot water, then cooled to room temperature

arabica filling (page 39)

*2 sandwich tins, 20 cm diameter, buttered and base-lined*

Serves 8

Put the butter into a bowl and, using a wooden spoon or electric mixer, beat until creamy. Beat in the sugar and continue beating until the mixture is light and fluffy. Break the eggs into a separate bowl and beat with a fork until slightly frothy. Gradually beat the eggs into the mixture, beating well after each addition. Sift the flour, cocoa and baking powder onto the mixture. Add the cool coffee and gently fold into the creamed mixture until blended. Spoon into the prepared tins and bake in a preheated oven at 180°C (350°F) Gas 4 for about 25–30 minutes until the sponge springs back when gently pressed in the centre. Turn out onto a wire rack, remove the paper and let cool completely before sandwiching and topping with arabica filling.

## speckled sponge

175 g unsalted butter, at room temperature

175 g caster sugar

3 large eggs, at room temperature

1 teaspoon vanilla essence

175 g self-raising flour

2 tablespoons milk

50 g plain chocolate, finely chopped, or chocolate chips

chocolate icing (pages 38–39)

*2 sandwich tins, 20 cm diameter, buttered and base-lined*

Serves 8

Put the butter into a bowl and, using a wooden spoon or electric mixer, beat until creamy. Beat in the sugar and continue beating until light and fluffy. Break the eggs into a separate bowl, add the vanilla essence and beat with a fork until slightly frothy. Gradually beat the eggs into the mixture, beating well after each addition. Sift the flour onto the mixture, add the milk and gently fold in until thoroughly blended. Stir in the chocolate. Spoon into the tins and bake in a preheated oven at 180°C (350°F) Gas 4 for 25–30 minutes until the sponge springs gently pressed in the centre. Turn out onto a wire rack, remove the lining paper and let cool. Layer and top with your chosen frosting.

# fillings and icings

### light and fluffy butter icing

Because it isn't too rich, this is an ideal icing for birthday cakes or children's party cakes.

125 g unsalted butter, at room temperature

400 g icing sugar, sifted

3 tablespoons cocoa powder, sifted

3–4 tablespoons milk

Makes enough to fill and top
1 sponge cake or top 24 fairy cakes

Put the butter into a bowl and, using a wooden spoon or electric mixer, beat until very soft and creamy. Gradually beat in the icing sugar, cocoa and milk to make a thick, smooth icing: if using an electric mixer, use low speed.

**Variations** To make a mocha icing, replace the milk with cold coffee. To make a white vanilla icing, omit the cocoa and beat in 1 teaspoon vanilla essence.

### sour cream filling and icing

Rich, silky-smooth and velvety.

180 g good-quality milk chocolate, finely chopped

90 g plain chocolate, finely chopped

225 ml sour cream

Makes enough to fill and top
1 sponge cake

Put both chocolates into a heatproof bowl set over a saucepan of steaming but not boiling water and melt gently (do not let the base of the bowl touch the water). Remove from the heat and stir gently until smooth. Using an electric hand whisk, whisk in the cream. The mixture will become thick and glossy. In cool conditions, the mixture will be spreadable immediately. In warm weather, chill for a few minutes until thick enough to spread. If the mixture becomes too hard, soften by setting the bowl briefly over a saucepan of steaming water.

### extra rich and creamy icing

Cream cheese gives a richer, heavier icing. For the ultimate vanilla icing, make up as below without the cocoa.

125 g unsalted butter, at room temperature

125 g cream cheese

1 teaspoon vanilla essence

450 g icing sugar, sifted

4 tablespoons cocoa powder, sifted

Makes enough to fill and top
1 sponge cake

Put the butter, cream cheese and vanilla into a mixing bowl and, using a wooden spoon or electric mixer, beat until soft and creamy. Gradually beat in the icing sugar and cocoa to make a thick, smooth mixture: if using an electric mixer, use low speed.

## arabica filling and icing

A French-style buttercream enriched with egg yolks. Add coffee to taste for a mild or more intense flavour. Decorate the finished cake with chocolate coffee beans for extra verve.

175 g unsalted butter, at room temperature
175 g icing sugar, sifted
2 large egg yolks
3 tablespoons espresso coffee or 3 teaspoons instant coffee dissolved in 3 tablespoons hot water (or to taste), then cooled to room temperature

Makes enough to fill and top
1 sponge cake

Put all the ingredients into a mixing bowl and, using a wooden spoon or electric mixer, beat until smooth, thick and creamy: if using an electric mixer, use low speed.

## fudge icing

A rich, very chocolaty topping for large cakes, loaf cakes, fairy cakes and cupcakes.

100 g plain chocolate, finely chopped
1 tablespoon golden syrup
25 g unsalted butter, at room temperature

Makes enough to fill and top
1 sponge cake or top 12 cupcakes

Put the chocolate into a heatproof bowl set over a saucepan of steaming water but not boiling water and melt gently (do not let the base of the bowl touch the water). Remove from the heat and stir in the golden syrup and butter. When smooth, let cool, stirring occasionally, until thick and on the point of setting. If the mixture sets before you are ready to use it, gently melt over very low heat. Spread over the cake and let set.

## ganache

The smoothest, least sweet chocolate icing is made from equal quantities of chocolate and double cream. For a softer icing, use a little more cream than chocolate: for a darker but harder covering, use a little more chocolate than cream.

115 ml double cream
110 g plain chocolate, finely chopped

Makes enough to fill and top
1 sponge cake

Put the cream into a saucepan and heat until scalding hot. Put the chocolate into a heatproof bowl, then pour over the hot cream. Leave for about 2 minutes, then stir until just smooth. Let cool until thick enough to spread.

This traditional German recipe is nothing like the commercial cakes on sale these days. This is the real thing (and note that the sponge contains no flour).

# black forest gâteau

**Chocolate sponge**

9 large eggs, separated

200 g caster sugar

90 g cocoa powder, sifted

**Cherry filling**

720 g jar or can of Morello cherries in kirsch syrup – or syrup plus 3 tablespoons kirsch (a 50 ml miniature)

425 ml double or whipping cream

3 tablespoons caster sugar

55 g plain chocolate, grated

*3 sandwich tins, 20 cm diameter, buttered and base-lined*

Serves 8–10

To make the sponge cakes, put the egg yolks and sugar into a bowl and, using an electric whisk or electric mixer, whisk until very thick and mousse-like – when the whisk is lifted, a wide ribbon-like trail slowly falls back into the bowl. Sift the cocoa onto the mixture and gently fold in with a large metal spoon.

Put the egg whites into a spotlessly clean, grease-free bowl and whisk, using an electric mixer, electric whisk or rotary whisk, until stiff peaks form. Carefully fold into the yolk mixture in 3 batches. Divide the mixture between the 3 prepared tins, then bake in a preheated oven at 180°C (350°F) Gas 4 for 20–25 minutes until the sponge cakes spring back when gently pressed, and have shrunk away from the sides of the tins. Let cool in the pans before turning out onto a wire rack and peeling off the lining paper.

Drain the cherries in a sieve and save the syrup: you will need 7 tablespoons (if using cherries in sugar syrup, put 4 tablespoons of the sugar syrup into a bowl and add the 3 tablespoons kirsch). When the cherries have been well drained, leave them on kitchen paper. Reserve 12 to decorate.

Set one of the cooled sponges onto a pretty serving plate, then sprinkle 2 tablespoons of the kirsch syrup over the sponge.

Put the cream into a bowl and, using an electric mixer or whisk, whip the cream until soft peaks form. Sprinkle the sugar over the cream and whip until slightly thicker. Set aside half the cream to cover the cake. Spread half the remaining cream onto the bottom layer of sponge. Press half the cherries into the cream. Sprinkle the second sponge layer with the kirsch syrup as before, then gently set on top of the first layer. Spread with cream and press in the cherries as before. Top with the final layer of sponge. Sprinkle with the remaining kirsch syrup. Cover the top and sides of the cake with the rest of the cream – you can either spread or pipe the cream – then decorate with the reserved cherries and grated chocolate. Chill until ready to serve. Best eaten within 48 hours.

My editor, Elsa Petersen-Schepelern, and her sister Kirsten are both great cooks, and Kirsten's chocolate cake is legendary – a fabulous combination of moist dark sponge, thick nutty filling and dark chocolate icing. An electric mixer will really help here.

# chocolate layer cake

55 g cocoa powder

300 g self-raising flour

¼ teaspoon salt

½ teaspoon baking powder

125 g unsalted butter, at room temperature

200 g caster sugar

3 large eggs, beaten

1 teaspoon vanilla essence

100 ml milk

Nutty filling

225 ml pure maple syrup

2 large egg whites

4 tablespoons chopped pecan nuts

Icing

3 tablespoons cocoa powder

15 g butter, at room temperature

1 tablespoon maple syrup

1 egg white

200 g icing sugar, sifted

3 sandwich tins, 20 cm diameter, buttered and base-lined

Serves 12

Sift the cocoa into a heatproof bowl, then stir in 125 ml boiling water to make a smooth paste. Let cool.

Sift the flour, salt and baking powder 3 times onto a sheet of greaseproof paper.

Put the butter into a bowl and, using a wooden spoon or an electric mixer, beat until creamy. Beat in the sugar thoroughly, until the mixture is light and fluffy. Gradually beat in the eggs and the vanilla, then gradually beat in the cooled cocoa mixture. Using a large metal spoon, fold in the flour mixture alternately with the milk. When thoroughly combined, divide the mixture evenly between the 3 prepared tins and spread evenly. Bake in a preheated oven at 190°C (375°F) Gas 5 for about 20 minutes, until just firm to the touch. Turn out onto a wire rack, remove the lining paper and let cool.

To make the filling, put the maple syrup into a medium, heavy-based saucepan and bring to the boil until it reaches 115°C (238°F) on a sugar thermometer (soft ball stage). This will take about 5 minutes: take care as the syrup can bubble up alarmingly if the heat is too high. While the syrup is heating, put the egg whites into a clean, grease-free bowl and whisk until stiff peaks form. When the syrup has reached the correct stage, pour it onto the egg whites in a thin steady stream, whisking constantly. Continue whisking until the mixture is very thick and fluffy. Stir in the chopped nuts, then use to sandwich and coat the cakes.

To make the icing, sift the cocoa into a heatproof bowl, add the butter and maple syrup, then stir in 125 ml boiling water to make a thick, smooth paste. Add the unbeaten egg white, then, using a wooden spoon or electric mixer, gradually beat in the icing sugar to make a thin, smooth, spreadable icing. Pour the icing over the cake and gently spread it so it covers the entire cake. Chill for a few minutes until firm, then serve at room temperature.

# sachertorte

The most famous of all the Viennese cakes, this sumptuous chocolate cake was invented in 1832 by the chef at the Hotel Sacher. At the hotel, you can still buy a sachertorte, made from the original recipe and packaged in a stylish wooden box.

175 g plain chocolate, finely chopped

125 g unsalted butter, at room temperature

150 g caster sugar

5 large eggs, plus 1 egg white

150 g plain flour

½ teaspoon baking powder

Apricot glaze

4 tablespoons apricot conserve

1 teaspoon lemon juice

Chocolate icing

125 ml double cream

175 g plain chocolate, chopped

a little melted milk chocolate, to pipe (optional)

whipped cream, to serve

*a springform or loose-based cake tin, 23 cm diameter, buttered and base-lined*

*a greaseproof paper piping bag (optional)*

Serves 12

1 Put the chocolate into a heatproof bowl set over a saucepan of steaming but not boiling water and melt gently (do not let the base of the bowl touch the water). Remove from the heat and let cool.

2 Put the butter into a large bowl and, using a wooden spoon or electric mixer, beat until creamy. Add half the sugar and beat until light and fluffy.

3 Separate the eggs. Put the 6 whites into a large, spotlessly clean and grease-free bowl.

Using an electric whisk or mixer, beat 5 of the yolks into the creamed mixture, one at a time, beating well after each addition. (Reserve the remaining yolk for another purpose.)

4 Stir in the cooled chocolate.

**5** Sift the flour and baking powder onto the mixture and gently fold in with a large metal spoon.

**6** Using an electric mixer or rotary whisk, whisk the egg whites until stiff peaks form, then beat in the remaining sugar 1 tablespoon at a time.

**7** Fold into the chocolate mixture in 3 batches.

**8** When the mixture is evenly blended, spoon into the prepared tin and level the surface. Bake in a preheated oven at 170°C (325°F) Gas 3 for 1 hour or until a skewer inserted in the centre comes out clean. Let cool in the tin for 10 minutes, then carefully turn out onto a wire rack, remove the lining paper and let cool completely. (The flat base will be easier to ice.)

**9** To make the glaze, put the apricot conserve, lemon juice and 1 tablespoon water into a small saucepan, heat gently, then bring gently to the boil, stirring constantly. Remove from the heat and push through a sieve into a bowl.

**10** Brush the hot glaze over the top and sides of the cake (the cake can also be split in half horizontally and sandwiched with extra glaze). Let cool on the wire rack.

**11** Meanwhile, to make the icing, put the cream into a small saucepan and heat until almost boiling. Put the chopped chocolate into a heatproof bowl and pour over the hot cream.

**12** Leave for 2 minutes, then stir until the icing is smooth and glossy.

**13** Put a plate under the wire rack to catch the drips, then pour the icing over the cake so it covers the top and sides – if necessary, spread the icing to cover any bare patches. Let set in a cool place, but not the refrigerator.

**14** If liked, put some melted chocolate into a greaseproof paper icing bag and pipe the word 'Sacher' or the letter 'S' on top of the cake.

Cut into small slices and serve with whipped cream. For best results, use a sharp knife and, before making each cut, dip the knife into hot water and wipe it dry. Store the cake in an airtight container in a cool place.

Best eaten within 1 week. The un-iced cake can be frozen for up to 1 month.

# black and white chocolate marble loaf cake

The classic English pound cake recipe (known as *quatre quarts* in France and *sandkuchen* in Germany), uses equal weights of butter, flour, sugar and eggs. It's very easy to turn the basic sponge mixture into an impressive, richly flavoured marbled loaf. Serve thick slices with a cup of tea or coffee. The cake is also perfect for picnics, but for a real treat, serve warm for pudding with plenty of whipped cream, custard or even Rich Dark Chocolate Sauce (page 106).

225 g unsalted butter, at room temperature

225 g golden caster sugar

4 large eggs, at room temperature, lightly beaten

1 teaspoon vanilla essence

225 g self-raising flour

75 g plain chocolate, chopped

1 tablespoon cocoa powder

75 g white chocolate, chopped

a loaf tin, 900 g, buttered and base-lined

Makes 1 large loaf

Put the butter into a large mixing bowl and, using a wooden spoon or electric mixer, beat until very creamy. Beat in the sugar and continue beating for about 2 minutes until the mixture is lighter in colour and consistency. Gradually beat in the eggs, then beat in the vanilla essence. Sift the flour onto the creamed mixture and gently fold in with a large metal spoon.

Spoon half the cake mixture into another mixing bowl. Put the plain chocolate into a heatproof bowl set over a saucepan of steaming but not boiling water and melt gently (do not let the base of the bowl touch the water). Remove the bowl from the heat and let cool. Sift the cocoa onto one portion of cake mixture, add the cooled melted plain chocolate, then, using a large metal spoon, carefully fold in until evenly mixed.

Put the white chocolate into a heatproof bowl set over a saucepan of steaming but not boiling water and melt gently (do not let the base of the bowl touch the water). Remove the bowl from the heat and let cool. Using a clean metal spoon, fold into the remaining portion of cake mixture.

Spoon both cake mixtures into the prepared tin, using each mixture alternately. To make the marbling, draw a knife through the mixtures and swirl together.

Bake in a preheated oven at 180°C (350°F) Gas 4 for about 1¼ hours or until a skewer inserted in the centre comes out clean. Turn out gently onto a wire rack, remove the lining paper and let cool completely.

Store in an airtight container. Best eaten within 5 days. The cake can be frozen for up to 1 month.

# pain d'épices au chocolat

The classic French *pain d'épices* – honey spice cake – should be made with equal weights of flour and honey, and flavoured with *quatre épices*, a ready-made mixture of spices usually available only in French food shops. The grated chocolate is a fairly new addition to the medieval recipe and replaces the traditional chopped almonds and candied peel. Try this cake, thickly sliced, with a cup of good coffee.

200 g unbleached plain flour

100 g rye flour

¼ teaspoon fine sea salt

2 teaspoons baking powder

½ teaspoon ground cinnamon

½ teaspoon ground cloves

½ teaspoon quatre épices*

100 g plain chocolate, grated or finely chopped

300 g well flavoured clear honey

2 large egg yolks

5 tablespoons milk

Chocolate glaze

50 g plain chocolate, chopped

2 tablespoons caster sugar

3 tablespoons milk

*a loaf tin, 450 g, buttered and base-lined*

Makes 1 medium loaf

Sift both the flours, salt, baking powder and all the spices into a mixing bowl. Stir in the grated chocolate. Add the honey, egg yolks and milk and mix with a wooden spoon to make a thick, heavy cake mixture. Spoon into the prepared tin and level the surface. Bake immediately in a preheated oven at 180°C (350°F) Gas 4 for about 45 minutes until the loaf turns golden brown and a skewer inserted in the centre comes out clean. Turn out onto a wire rack and remove the lining paper.

As soon as the loaf is out of the oven, make the glaze. Put the chocolate, sugar and milk into a small, heavy-based saucepan and heat gently, stirring, until the chocolate has melted. Bring to the boil, still stirring, let bubble for about 5 seconds, then remove from the heat. Pour, spoon or brush the hot, thin glaze over the warm loaf and let it drip down the sides. Leave the loaf until completely cold before slicing. Store in an airtight container.

Best eaten within 5 days. The unglazed loaf can be frozen for up to 1 month.

**\*Note** To make *quatre épices*, the late Jane Grigson suggested mixing 7 parts finely ground black pepper with 1 part each of ground cloves, ground ginger and grated nutmeg. Store in a screw-top jar.

As with the perfect Brownie recipe, finding the ultimate Devil's Food Cake involved years of tasting. Once again, my mother-in-law in Maine came up with a lovely recipe. It does seem a bit odd, but it works – and the final result is a very light textured sponge, properly dark in colour and with a great flavour.

# devil's food cake

110 g plain chocolate, finely chopped

125 ml sour cream

175 g light muscovado sugar

300 g plain flour

a good pinch of salt

3 tablespoons cocoa powder

1 teaspoon bicarbonate of soda

115 g unsalted butter, at room temperature

200 g caster sugar

2 large eggs, separated

1 teaspoon vanilla essence

175 ml water, at room temperature

Icing and filling

140 g plain chocolate, finely chopped

140 g milk chocolate, finely chopped

225 ml sour cream

3 sponge tins, 20 cm diameter, or 2 sponge tins, 23 cm diameter, buttered and base-lined

Serves 10–12

Put the chopped chocolate, sour cream and muscovado sugar into a heavy-based saucepan and set over very low heat. Stir occasionally until melted and smooth but don't let the mixture become hot. Remove from the heat and set aside until needed.

Sift the flour with the salt, cocoa and bicarbonate of soda onto a sheet of greaseproof paper and set aside.

Put the butter into a bowl and, using a wooden spoon or electric whisk, beat until creamy. Gradually beat in the caster sugar. Beat well, then beat in the egg yolks one at a time, followed by the vanilla essence. Mix in the flour mixture, 1 tablespoon at a time, alternately with the water (if using the mixer, use low speed and mix as little as possible). When thoroughly blended, work in the melted chocolate mixture. Spoon the mixture into the prepared tins, to fill evenly, then bake in a preheated oven at 180°C (350°F) Gas 4 for 25 minutes for the smaller cakes or 30 minutes for the larger ones. The cakes are cooked when they spring back when gently pressed in the centre and have slightly shrunk away from the sides of the tins. Let cool for 5 minutes, then invert onto a wire rack, remove the lining paper and cool completely.

To make the icing and filling, put the plain and milk chocolates into a heatproof bowl set over a saucepan of steaming but not boiling water and leave until melted (do not let the base of the bowl touch the water). Remove the bowl from the heat, stir gently until smooth, then whisk in the cream. Leave until very thick and spreadable (in hot weather you may need to chill it briefly).

Set one cake aside and spread icing on top of the remaining cake(s). Sandwich the layers together, with the plain one on top. Spread the top and sides of the cake with icing. (In hot weather, chill the cake for a few minutes until the icing is firm.) Keep in a cool place until ready to serve.

The un-iced cake may be stored in an airtight container for up to 24 hours. The finished cake is best eaten within 5 days. The un-iced cakes can be frozen for up to 1 month.

Cut into this chocolate covered cake and you will find a rich, tangy orange sponge interior. Serve as an afternoon treat or as a pudding with piles of whipped cream or scoops of vanilla or chocolate ice cream (page 110).

# surprise cake

175 g unsalted butter, at room temperature

175 g golden caster sugar

grated zest of 2 unwaxed oranges

3 large eggs, beaten

175 g self-raising flour, sifted

2 tablespoons fresh orange juice (from about ½ orange)

Orange syrup

100 ml freshly squeezed orange juice (from about 1½ oranges)

1–2 tablespoons orange liqueur, such as Cointreau or Grand Marnier (optional)

85 g golden caster sugar

Chocolate icing

150 g plain chocolate, finely chopped

55 g unsalted butter, cut into small pieces

*a springform or deep cake tin, 20 cm diameter, buttered and base-lined*

Serves 8

Put the butter into a mixing bowl and, using a wooden spoon or electric mixer, beat until creamy. Add the sugar and the orange zest and beat until light and fluffy. Gradually beat in the eggs, beating well after each addition. Using a large metal spoon, fold in the flour in 3 batches, adding the orange juice with the last batch of flour. Spoon the batter into the prepared tin and level the surface. Bake in a preheated oven at 180°C (350°F) Gas 4 for 35–40 minutes.

While the cake is baking, make the orange syrup. Put the orange juice (if using liqueur, replace 1–2 tablespoons of the orange juice with liqueur) and caster sugar into a bowl and, using a large metal spoon, mix until the sugar dissolves.

As soon as the cake is well risen, golden brown and a skewer inserted in the centre comes out clean, remove from the oven and transfer to a wire rack (do not turn it out of the tin). Prick the cake all over with a skewer or cocktail stick and slowly spoon the orange syrup over the cake, until it has all been absorbed. Leave until cold before removing from the tin and removing the lining paper.

To make the icing, put the chocolate and butter into a heatproof bowl set over a saucepan of steaming but not boiling water and melt gently (do not let the base of the bowl touch the water). Remove the bowl from the heat, gently stir the chocolate until smooth, then spread it evenly over the top and sides of the cake. Let set, then transfer to a serving plate. Store in an airtight container.

Best eaten within 6 days. The cooled cake, minus the syrup, can be frozen for up to 1 month. Defrost the cake, then gently warm the syrup, pour over the cake and finish as in the main recipe.

It's a shame to keep fruit cakes just for Christmas and weddings. This one is simple, fairly light and easy to make for a weekend party. With a combination of almond sponge, glacé cherries (the naturally coloured ones are best), the largest and juiciest raisins you can find, walnut halves and chunks of plain chocolate, there's no need for an icing or topping.

# chocolate fruit and nut cake

150 g large seedless raisins

75 g glacé cherries, halved

2 tablespoons rum, orange juice or cold tea

225 g unsalted butter, at room temperature

225 g caster sugar

4 large eggs, at room temperature, beaten

225 g plain flour

1 tablespoon baking powder

a pinch of salt

85 g ground almonds

100 g plain chocolate, coarsely chopped

100 g walnut pieces

a springform or deep cake tin, 22 cm diameter, buttered and base-lined

Serves 10

Put the raisins, cherries and rum into a small bowl, stir, then cover with clingfilm and let soak for at least 2 hours, preferably overnight.

Put the butter into a mixing bowl and, using a wooden spoon or electric mixer, beat until creamy. Add the sugar and beat until light and fluffy. Gradually beat in the eggs. Sift the flour, baking powder, salt and ground almonds onto the creamed mixture, and using a large metal spoon, fold the dry ingredients into the mixture. Add the fruit and rum mixture, the chopped chocolate and walnuts and gently stir in until thoroughly blended. Spoon the mixture into the prepared tin and level the surface.

Bake in a preheated oven at 180°C (350°F) Gas 4 for 1–1¼ hours until the top is golden brown, firm to the touch and a skewer inserted into the centre comes out clean. Let cool in the tin, then invert onto a wire rack, remove the lining paper and cool completely. Wrap in greaseproof paper and keep overnight before cutting. Store in an airtight container.

Best eaten within 1 week. Can be frozen for up to 1 month.

This is what I make when we need a treat – warm, slightly soft brownies packed with nuts, topped with a few shavings of white chocolate or a scoop of vanilla ice cream and lots of hot, very chocolaty fudge sauce. The combination of the contrasting textures, temperatures and tastes is truly sublime.

# fudge brownies with chocolate fudge sauce

100 g plain chocolate, finely chopped

125 g unsalted butter, at room temperature

275 g caster sugar

1 teaspoon vanilla essence

2 large eggs, beaten

85 g plain flour

2 tablespoons cocoa powder

a pinch of salt

100 g pecan halves or walnut pieces

### Chocolate fudge sauce

175 g plain chocolate, finely chopped

40 g unsalted butter

2 tablespoons caster sugar

2 tablespoons golden syrup

175 ml milk or single cream

*a cake tin, 20 cm square, buttered and base-lined*

Makes 16

Put the chocolate into a heatproof bowl set over a saucepan of steaming but not boiling water and melt gently (do not let the base of the bowl touch the water). Remove the bowl from the heat and let cool while making the mixture.

Put the butter into a large mixing bowl and, using a wooden spoon or electric mixer, beat until soft and creamy. Add the sugar and vanilla essence and continue beating until the mixture is soft and fluffy. Gradually beat in the eggs.

Sift the flour, cocoa and salt onto the mixture, then spoon the melted chocolate on top and gently stir together until thoroughly mixed. Stir in the nuts. Spoon the mixture into the prepared tin and level the surface.

Bake in a preheated oven at 180°C (350°F) Gas 4 for 30–35 minutes until a skewer inserted halfway between the sides of the tin and the centre comes out clean – it is important that the centre is just set but still slightly soft and not cake-like. Let cool in the tin, then remove from the tin and cut into 16 squares. Eat warm or at room temperature with the chocolate sauce. When cold, the brownies may be stored in an airtight container.

To make the chocolate sauce, put all the ingredients into a small, heavy-based saucepan and set over low heat. Stir gently until melted and smooth. Continue heating and stirring until the mixture is almost at boiling point. Remove from the heat and serve immediately. The sauce will thicken as it cools.

The brownies are best eaten within 5 days, or can be frozen for up to 1 month. The chocolate sauce is best eaten the same day or, when cool, cover with clingfilm and store in the refrigerator for up to 48 hours. Reheat gently.

*Note  To make removal easier, I cut the parchment paper wider, so it overlaps the edges of the pan. After cooling, remove the uncut slab of brownies using the overlapping paper as handles. Work gently, to avoid cracking the top.

A cross between scones, rock cakes and American shortcake, these muffins are rich, moist and very crumbly. Eat warm – there is no need to serve them with butter.

# chocolate crumble muffins

250 g self-raising flour

a pinch of salt

85 g caster sugar

85 g unsalted butter, chilled and cut into small pieces

75 g plain chocolate, grated or finely chopped

50 g finely chopped nuts (optional)

2 tablespoons very finely chopped mixed peel

1 large egg

about 175 ml single cream

chocolate chips or almonds, to decorate

*a 12-hole muffin tin, lined with paper muffin cases or well buttered*

Makes 12

Sift the flour, salt and sugar into a mixing bowl. Add the butter and, using the tips of your fingers, rub in until the mixture resembles fine breadcrumbs. Stir in the chocolate, nuts and mixed peel. Break the egg into a measuring jug, then add enough cream to make 230 ml. Add the egg mixture to the bowl and mix with a round-bladed knife until the dough comes together – it will be quite sticky.

Divide the dough equally between the prepared muffin cases, then decorate with chocolate chips or almonds.

Bake in a preheated oven at 220°C (425°F) Gas 7 for 10 minutes, then reduce the heat to 180°C (350°F) Gas 4 and bake for a further 5–10 minutes or until golden brown and firm to the touch. Remove from the oven and let cool on a wire rack. When completely cold, store in an airtight container.

Best eaten within 2 days. Can be frozen for up to 1 month.

Making doughnuts is something I do on impulse on a gloomy winter's afternoon. I prefer to use a rich, scone-like dough rather than a yeast dough, as much for the taste and very light texture as for the instant gratification. The icing is rich and glossy, but if you prefer sugar-coated doughnuts, roll the hot doughnuts in caster sugar mixed with a little ground cinnamon. The buttermilk can be replaced with 3 tablespoons plain yoghurt made up to 90 ml with milk.

# chocolate doughnuts

60 g unsalted butter, very soft

60 g caster sugar

1 large egg, lightly beaten

90 ml buttermilk

225 g plain flour

1 teaspoon baking powder

½ teaspoon bicarbonate of soda

20 g cocoa powder

¼ teaspoon salt

1 teaspoon ground cinnamon

several gratings of fresh nutmeg

peanut or sunflower oil, for deep-frying

Chocolate icing

75 g plain chocolate, finely chopped

75 g icing sugar, sifted

2 round biscuit cutters,
2.5 cm and 8 cm

Makes 8

Put the butter, sugar, egg and buttermilk into a large mixing bowl. Sift the flour, baking powder, bicarbonate of soda, cocoa, salt and spices on top and, using a wooden spoon or electric mixer (on low speed), mix until the ingredients are thoroughly blended. Turn the mixture out onto a floured work surface and knead gently to make a smooth dough – slightly soft but not sticky, rather like a scone dough. If necessary work in a little more flour.

Using floured hands, pat out the dough about 1.5 cm thick. Cut out discs using the 8 cm cutter, then stamp out the centres with the smaller cutter. Knead the trimmings together, then use to make more doughnuts.

Fill a chip pan one-third full with the oil (or an electric deep-fat fryer to the manufacturer's recommended level). Heat the oil to 180°C (350°F) or until a small cube of bread will brown in 40 seconds. Fry the doughnuts 2–3 at a time, turning them frequently until darker brown and cooked through, about 4 minutes. Using a slotted spoon, remove from the oil and drain on kitchen paper.

While the doughnuts are cooling, make the icing. Put the chocolate into a heatproof bowl set over a saucepan of steaming but not boiling water and melt gently (do not let the base of the bowl touch the water). Remove the bowl from the heat and stir in the sugar and 4 tablespoons hot water to make a smooth, runny icing. Dip the tops of the doughnuts in the icing and leave on a wire rack until set.

Best eaten the same day.

# crescent moons

110 g unsalted butter,
at room temperature

2–3 drops almond essence

60 g icing sugar, sifted

a pinch of salt

85 g plain flour, sifted

120 g ground almonds

To finish

50 g plain chocolate, melted

icing sugar, for sprinkling

*several baking sheets, buttered*

*non-stick baking parchment*

Makes about 24

Put the butter and almond essence into a mixing bowl and, using a wooden spoon or electric mixer, beat until very soft and creamy. Gradually beat in the icing sugar, on slow speed if using an electric mixer, then beat well until very fluffy. Work in the salt, flour and ground almonds and, if necessary, knead gently to bring the dough together. Wrap in clingfilm and chill for about 20 minutes until firm.

Take a heaped teaspoon of dough and roll it with your hands into a sausage shape about 7 cm long, then curve it to make a crescent. Repeat with the rest of dough and set the crescents well apart on the prepared baking sheets. Bake in a preheated oven at 170°C (325°F) Gas 3 for 15–18 minutes until just firm, but still pale with just the very edges slightly coloured. Remove from the oven and let cool on the trays for about 2 minutes or until firm enough to transfer to a wire rack to cool completely.

When cold, dip one end of each crescent into the melted chocolate, then transfer to non-stick baking parchment. Leave in a cool place until set, then sprinkle the plain end with icing sugar. Store in an airtight container.

Best eaten within 1 week. Not suitable for freezing.

# double chocolate macaroons

75 g plain chocolate, chopped

2 large egg whites,
at room temperature

200 g caster sugar

125 g ground almonds

2–3 drops almond essence

Chocolate filling

110 g white chocolate, chopped

100 ml double cream

*2 baking sheets, lined with*
*non-stick baking parchment*

Makes 8 pairs

Put the plain chocolate into a heatproof bowl set over a saucepan of steaming but not boiling water and melt gently (do not let the base of the bowl touch the water). Remove the bowl from the heat and stir until smooth. Let cool while making the rest of the mixture. Put the egg whites into a spotlessly clean, grease-free bowl and, using an electric whisk or mixer, whisk until stiff peaks form. Gradually whisk in the sugar to make a thick, glossy meringue. Using a large metal spoon, fold in the ground almonds, almond essence and melted chocolate. When thoroughly blended, put 1 tablespoon of the mixture onto the prepared baking sheet and spread to a disc about 5 cm across. Repeat with the rest of the mixture, spacing the macaroons well apart.

Bake in a preheated oven at 150°C (300°F) Gas 2 for 30 minutes until just firm. Remove from the oven and let cool on the trays for about 2 minutes or until firm enough to transfer to a wire rack to cool completely. When cold, peel the macaroons away from the lining paper.

To make the filling, put the white chocolate and cream into a small, heavy-based saucepan and heat very gently, stirring occasionally, until melted and smooth. Remove from the heat, let cool, then, using a wooden spoon, beat until thick and fluffy. Use to sandwich the macaroons together and set aside for at least 1 hour before serving. Store in an airtight container.

Best eaten within 5 days. Not suitable for freezing.

# giant double chocolate nut cookies

140 g plain chocolate, chopped

100 g unsalted butter, at room temperature

80 g golden caster sugar

80 g dark brown muscovado sugar

1 large egg, beaten

½ teaspoon vanilla essence

150 g plain flour

a pinch of salt

½ teaspoon baking powder

50 g pecan nuts or walnuts, chopped

100 g plain or white chocolate, chopped into chunks

*several baking sheets, buttered*

Makes 16

Chocolate chip cookies with a difference – double chocolate. The chips are chunks of plain or white chocolate, and the mixture is flavoured with melted chocolate.

Put the chopped chocolate into a heatproof bowl set over a saucepan of barely simmering water and melt gently (do not let the base of the bowl touch the water). Remove the bowl from the heat and let cool. Meanwhile, using a wooden spoon or electric mixer, beat the butter until creamy. Add the sugars and beat again until light and fluffy. Gradually beat in the egg and vanilla essence, followed by the melted chocolate. Sift the flour, salt and baking powder into the bowl and stir. When thoroughly mixed, work in the nuts and chocolate chunks. Put heaped tablespoons of the mixture, spaced well apart, onto the prepared baking sheets.

Bake in a preheated oven at 180°C (350°F) Gas 4 for 12–15 minutes until just firm. Remove from the oven and let cool on the trays for 2 minutes or until firm enough to transfer to a wire rack. Let cool completely, then store in an airtight container.

Best eaten within 1 week. Can be frozen for up to 1 month.

# black and white cookies

115 g unsalted butter, at room temperature

85 g light brown muscovado sugar

1 large egg, beaten

60 g self-raising flour

½ teaspoon baking powder

a pinch of salt

½ teaspoon vanilla essence

115 g porridge oats

175 g plain chocolate, chopped into chunks

*several baking sheets, buttered*

Makes about 24

These cookies are my all-time favourites. For best results, use coarsely chopped plain chocolate rather than chocolate chips.

Put the butter into a large mixing bowl and, using a wooden spoon or electric mixer, beat until creamy. Add the sugar and beat until light and creamy. Gradually beat in the egg, and beat well after the last addition. Sift the flour, baking powder and salt into the bowl, add the vanilla essence and oats, and stir in. When thoroughly mixed, stir in the chocolate chunks.

Put heaped teaspoons of the mixture, spaced well apart, onto the prepared baking sheets, then bake in a preheated oven at 180°C (350°F) Gas 4 for 12–15 minutes until golden and just firm. Remove from the oven and let cool on the sheets for about 2 minutes or until firm enough to transfer to a wire rack. Let cool completely, then store in an airtight container.

Best eaten within 1 week. Can be frozen for up to 1 month.

Keep a bag of these tiny, buttery buns in the freezer for lazy breakfasts. Warm through and eat with steaming cups of coffee or hot chocolate (page 121). The dough is simpler to make than the traditional brioche recipe, particularly using an electric mixer fitted with a dough hook – and the dough can be left to rise overnight in the refrigerator. You can also vary the flavour and texture by chopping the chocolate very finely or into larger chunks.

# petites brioches

500 g unbleached strong white bread flour, plus extra for dusting

1 teaspoon sea salt

100 g unsalted butter, cut into small pieces

50 g caster sugar

250 ml milk, lukewarm

15 g fresh yeast or 1 sachet (7 g) easy-blend dried yeast*

1 large egg, beaten

1 teaspoon vanilla essence

150 g plain chocolate, finely or coarsely chopped

50 g pine nuts, lightly toasted

1 egg, beaten, to glaze

*12 individual brioche moulds, 8 cm diameter, or 2 medium brioche moulds, 16.5 cm diameter, or 2 loaf tins, 450 g each, well buttered*

Makes 12 tiny brioches or 2 medium brioches or loaves

* To use easy-blend dried yeast, add the contents of one 7 g sachet to the flour with the sugar and mix well. Add the liquids and finish as in main recipe.

Put the flour and salt into a large mixing bowl and stir well. Add the butter and, using the tips of your fingers, rub into the flour until the mixture resembles breadcrumbs. Stir in the sugar*, then make a well in the centre.

Put the milk into a bowl and crumble the fresh yeast over the top. Stir until smooth, then stir in the egg and vanilla essence. Pour the mixture into the well in the flour. Using the dough hook of an electric mixer and low speed, gradually mix the flour into the liquids to make a soft and slightly sticky dough. On low speed, knead the dough for about 5 minutes or until smooth, elastic, shiny and soft. If the dough still sticks to the sides of the bowl, work in a little extra flour, 1 tablespoon at a time.

If making the dough by hand, put it onto a well floured work surface and knead for 10 minutes until smooth, elastic and shiny. If it is difficult to work, add a little extra flour. Return the dough to the cleaned out bowl, then slip it into a large plastic bag and let rise in a warm place until doubled in size – 1½ hours, or overnight in the refrigerator.

Punch down the dough with your knuckles and invert onto a floured work surface. Pat out to a large rectangle, then sprinkle over the chocolate and pine nuts. Fold or roll up, flatten and repeat twice until the chocolate and nuts are evenly distributed.

Cut the dough into 12 even portions for individual brioches or into 2 for large ones. Shape the 12 portions into balls and put one into each mould. For large ones, cut one-quarter off each portion of dough for the top and set aside. Shape the larger piece into a ball and put into the mould. Using 2 fingers, make a hole in the centre. Roll the smaller piece of dough into a ball, then into an egg shape. Push the narrow end into the hole. For a loaf, scoop the dough into the tins. Put into a plastic bag and let rise in a warm place until doubled in size – 1 hour, or overnight in the refrigerator.

Uncover the dough, brush with beaten egg, then bake in a preheated oven at 200°C (400°F) Gas 6 until well risen and golden brown – 15 minutes for individual brioches, 35 minutes for large ones. Turn out onto a wire rack and let cool. Eat warm.

Can be frozen for up to 1 month.

# puddings

I can't stop myself smiling when something chocolate appears on the table to round off a meal. Tarts and pies, mousses and soufflés – there's a chocolate pudding for every season (and, if you use really good quality cocoa powder, it will deliver real flavour without any extra sugar or fat).

# very rich chocolate brûlée

Steve Painter, fellow chocolate fiend and the designer of this book, insisted I include this recipe, which he makes often. The smooth chocolate cream can be made up to 2 days ahead, with the crunchy caramel topping added just before serving. You need a really hot grill or a cook's blowtorch, available from kitchen suppliers (page 126) for the best mirror-like finish.

600 ml double cream

1 vanilla pod, split lengthways*

300 g plain chocolate, chopped

4 large egg yolks

60 g icing sugar, sifted

about 4 tablespoons caster sugar, for sprinkling

*8 small soufflé dishes or ramekins, 150 ml each*

*a bain-marie or roasting tin*

Serves 8

Pour the cream into a heavy-based saucepan and add the vanilla pod. Heat gently until just too hot for your finger to bear. Cover with a lid and leave to infuse for about 30 minutes.

Lift out the vanilla pod and, using a tip of a knife, scrape the seeds into the cream. Gently reheat the cream, then remove from the heat and stir in the chopped chocolate. When melted and smooth, let cool slightly.

Meanwhile, put the egg yolks and the icing sugar into a mixing bowl, beat with a wooden spoon until well blended, then stir in the just warm chocolate cream. Pour into the soufflé dishes, then stand the dishes in a bain-marie (a roasting tin half-filled with warm water). Cook in a preheated oven at 180°C (350°F) Gas 4 for about 30 minutes until just firm. Remove from the bain-marie and let cool, then cover and chill overnight or for up to 48 hours.

When ready to serve, heat the grill to maximum and half-fill the bain-marie or roasting tin with ice cubes and water. Sprinkle the tops of the chocolate creams with caster sugar, then set the soufflé dishes in the icy water (this prevents the chocolate melting) and quickly flash under the grill or with a blowtorch until the sugar melts and caramelizes. Eat within 1 hour.

*Note The vanilla pod can be replaced with 1 tablespoon dark rum, added to the mixture at the same time as the egg yolks.

# nut and chocolate strudel

An irresistible combination of filo pastry, nuts and rich dark chocolate makes this pudding a firm favourite at every dinner party. Serve with plenty of whipped cream. For best results, use only good quality chocolate and very fresh nuts and, before using the filo pastry, make sure it's properly thawed out, according to the instructions on the packet.

100 g blanched almonds

100 g shelled unsalted pistachios

100 g walnut pieces

75 g unsalted butter

75 g light muscovado sugar

75 g plain chocolate

200 g filo pastry, thawed if frozen

whipped cream, to serve

### Cinnamon syrup

110 g caster sugar

1 cinnamon stick

1 teaspoon lemon juice

2 tablespoons clear honey

*a large roasting tin, well buttered*

Serves 6–8

Put all the nuts into a food processor and chop until they resemble coarse breadcrumbs. Put the nuts into a heavy-based, dry frying pan and stir over low heat until just starting to colour. Because nuts scorch quickly, it's best to undercook slightly, rather than risk overcooking them. Remove from the heat and stir in the butter and sugar. Let cool. Using a sharp knife, chop the chocolate the same size as the chopped nuts, then mix with the nuts.

Unwrap the filo pastry and put onto a clean work surface. Overlap the sheets to make a large rectangle about 90 x 65 cm.

Sprinkle the filling evenly over the pastry, then carefully roll up. Arrange in a horseshoe shape in the prepared roasting tin, tucking the ends under neatly. Bake in a preheated oven at 180°C (350°F) Gas 4 for about 25 minutes or until the top is crisp and light golden brown. Remove from the oven and let cool in the tin while making the syrup.

To make the cinnamon syrup, put the sugar and 100 ml water into a medium, heavy-based saucepan and heat gently, stirring frequently, until dissolved. Bring to the boil, then add the cinnamon stick, lemon juice and honey and simmer for 10 minutes until syrupy. Let cool for 5 minutes, then remove the cinnamon stick and pour the hot syrup over the strudel. Let cool so the strudel can absorb the syrup, then cut into thick slices and serve with piles of whipped cream.

Best eaten within 24 hours. Not suitable for freezing.

# easy chocolate and berry roulade

A splendid stand-by pudding for a special dinner when time is tight. The roulade is a simple all-in-one cake mix, made with an electric mixer or hand beaters, baked in 8 minutes and filled with crème fraîche mixed with conserve and fresh berries.

110 g caster sugar

2 large eggs

50 g unsalted butter, very soft

100 g self-raising flour

3 tablespoons cocoa powder

1 teaspoon vanilla essence

## Cream filling

4 tablespoons blackberry conserve

200 g crème fraîche

250 g fresh blackberries, picked over to clean

## To serve

icing sugar, for sprinkling

chocolate curls (page 15)

*a Swiss roll tin or baking sheet, about 20 x 30 cm, buttered and lined with non-stick baking parchment*

Serves 6–8

*You can vary the fruit, depending on what's in season. I also make it with raspberries, strawberries, blueberries, dark cherries (pitted), all with their matching conserves.

**1** Put the sugar, eggs and butter into a mixing bowl, or the bowl of an electric mixer. Sift the flour and cocoa into the bowl, then add the vanilla essence and 2 tablespoons warm water.

**2** Whisk for about 1 minute or until you have a smooth, thick and creamy cake batter.

**3** Pour the mixture into the prepared tin.

**4** Spread it evenly with a spatula.

**5** Bake in a preheated oven at 200°C (400°F) Gas 6 for 8 minutes or until the mixture is well risen and just springy when you press it with your finger. Let cool in the tin for about 1 minute.

**6** Put a sheet of non-stick baking parchment on a work surface and sprinkle heavily with icing sugar.

**7** Turn the sponge out onto the baking parchment, then peel off the lining paper.

**8** Carefully roll up the sponge with the parchment inside, like a Swiss roll. Cover with the damp tea towel and leave on the wire rack until completely cold.

**9** Put the conserve and crème fraîche into a bowl and, using a metal spoon, fold gently together.

**10**  Carefully unroll the sponge. Don't worry if it has cracked – it will still look and taste good.

**11**  Spread the cream mixture over the sponge.

**12**  Sprinkle the berries evenly over the top.

**13**  Roll up the sponge fairly loosely and set on a large serving plate. Cover and chill until ready to serve – I prefer the texture the next day.

**14**  Just before serving, sprinkle with icing sugar and decorate with chocolate curls.

Best eaten within 48 hours. Not suitable for freezing.

easy chocolate and berry roulade  79

These thick, crisp, batter cakes are cooked by street vendors in Holland (the name comes from the Dutch *wafel*), Belgium and Northern France (where they are called *gaufres*). Pilgrims from Northern Europe took the recipe to America, where waffle parties became very popular in the 18th century. The honeycomb or grid pattern of the waffle is perfect for holding lashings of whipped cream, maple syrup, melted butter or peanut butter. My recipe comes from my American husband's family where, apparently, it has been made most weekends for 75 years. My son invented the chocolate version. You will need an electric or stove-top waffle iron for cooking these waffles.

## chocolate waffles

200 g plain flour

a good pinch of salt

50 g cocoa powder

2 teaspoons baking powder

3½ tablespoons caster sugar

2 large eggs, separated

400 ml milk

1 teaspoon vanilla essence

40 g unsalted butter, melted

icing sugar, for sprinkling

*a waffle iron or electric waffle maker, well buttered (see recipe method)*

Makes 10 waffles, about 14 cm across

Grease the waffle iron or electric waffle maker (consult the manufacturer's instructions if using for the first time), then heat. Depending on the type of waffle maker* or waffle iron, it may be necessary to brush it well again with oil or melted butter, using a non-plastic brush.

Sift the flour, salt, cocoa, baking powder and caster sugar into a mixing bowl and make a well in the centre. Add the egg yolks, milk, vanilla essence and melted butter to the well and, using a whisk, beat until just blended. Then gradually whisk the dry mixture into the liquids to make a thick, smooth batter.

Put the egg whites into a spotlessly clean, grease-free bowl and, using an electric mixer or rotary whisk, whisk until stiff peaks form. Using a large metal spoon, fold the egg whites into the batter until it looks evenly foamy – it is better to have streaks than to overmix at this point.

Using the large metal spoon, spoon in enough batter to fill the hot waffle iron, then close. Cook for 30 seconds over medium heat, then turn over the iron and cook the other side in the same way. Serve hot from the iron, sprinkled with plenty of icing sugar.

**Note** If using an electric waffle maker, follow the manufacturer's guidelines, but note that chocolate waffles will scorch quicker than plain ones.

An individual white chocolate sponge pudding, baked with a hidden centre of molten chocolate and served with whipped cream or a chocolate sauce (page 106), is perfect for any occasion. It is very important to use the best quality white and plain chocolate you can find.

# white and black puddings

**Dark chocolate filling**

75 g plain chocolate, chopped

80 ml double cream

**White chocolate sponge**

100 g white chocolate, chopped

175 g unsalted butter,
at room temperature

150 g golden caster sugar

3 large eggs, beaten

250 g self-raising flour

a pinch of salt

½ teaspoon vanilla essence

about 4 tablespoons milk

*an ice cube tray, oiled*

*6 small pudding moulds,
7.5 cm diameter, well buttered*

Serves 6

The chocolate filling should be made at least 1 hour before making the sponge (though the filling can be kept in the freezer for up to 1 week). Put the chocolate into a heatproof bowl set over a saucepan of steaming but not boiling water and melt gently (do not let the base of the bowl touch the water). Remove the bowl from the heat and stir gently until just smooth. Stir in the cream, then pour into the prepared ice cube tray to make 6 'cubes'. Freeze for at least 1 hour.

When ready to make the pudding, put the white chocolate into a heatproof bowl set over a saucepan of steaming but not boiling water and melt gently (do not let the base of the bowl touch the water). Remove the bowl from the heat, stir gently until just smooth, then let cool.

Put the butter into a large mixing bowl and, using a wooden spoon or electric mixer, beat the butter until creamy, then gradually beat in the sugar. When the mixture is very light and fluffy, beat in the eggs 1 tablespoon at a time, beating well after each addition. Using a large metal spoon, carefully fold in the flour and salt, followed by the melted chocolate, vanilla essence and just enough milk to give the mixture a firm dropping consistency. Spoon the mixture into the prepared moulds to fill by about half. Turn out the dark chocolate cubes, put one into the centre of each mould, then top up with more sponge mixture so each one is three-quarters full.

Stand the moulds in a roasting tin, then cover loosely with well-buttered foil. Bake in a preheated oven at 180°C (350°F) Gas 4 for about 25 minutes or until just firm to the touch. Run a round-bladed knife inside each mould to loosen the puddings, then carefully turn out onto individual plates. Serve immediately.

This delicious soufflé, with its exceedingly light and meltingly soft texture, is more like a hot chocolate mousse. The recipe is easy though – if you can make meringue you can make this soufflé. Serve with crisp biscuits, such as the Crescent Moons on page 64.

# chocolate soufflé

180 g plain chocolate, chopped

150 ml double cream

3 large eggs, separated

2 tablespoons Cognac or brandy

2 large egg whites

about 1 tablespoon softened butter, for the soufflé dishes

3 tablespoons caster sugar, plus extra for the soufflé dishes

icing sugar, for sprinkling

*4 soufflé dishes, 300 ml each, or 4 large coffee cups, buttered and sugared (see recipe method)*

*a baking sheet or roasting tin*

Serves 4

Brush the soufflé dishes with a little melted butter, then sprinkle with sugar to give an even coating. Stand the dishes on a baking sheet or in a roasting tin.

Put the chocolate into a medium, heavy-based saucepan, pour in the cream, then set over very low heat and stir frequently until melted and smooth. Remove from the heat and stir in the egg yolks, one at a time, followed by the Cognac. At this point the mixture can be covered and set aside for up to 2 hours.

Put the 5 egg whites into a spotlessly clean, grease-free bowl and, using an electric whisk or mixer, whisk until stiff peaks form. Gradually whisk in the caster sugar to give a glossy, stiff meringue. The chocolate mixture should feel comfortably warm to your finger, so gently reheat if necessary. Using a large metal spoon, add a little of the meringue to the chocolate mixture and mix thoroughly. This loosens the consistency, making it easier to incorporate the rest of the meringue. Pour the chocolate mixture on top of the remaining meringue and gently fold both mixtures together until just blended.

Spoon or pour the mixture into the prepared soufflé dishes – the mixture should come to just below the rim. Bake in a preheated oven at 220°C (425°F) Gas 7 for 8–10 minutes until barely set – the centres should be soft, and wobble when gently shaken. Sprinkle with icing sugar and eat immediately.

### Variations

**Chocolate, Prune and Armagnac Soufflé** Omit the Cognac. Substitute 8 large pitted Agen or mi-cuit prunes soaked overnight in 4 tablespoons Armagnac. Chop the prunes coarsely, then stir them, together with any remaining liquid, into the chocolate mixture.

**Chocolate Amaretti Soufflé** Omit the Cognac. Set an amaretti biscuit into each prepared soufflé dish. Spoon over 1 teaspoon Amaretto liqueur, then add the chocolate soufflé mixture and bake as in the main recipe.

# classic chocolate mousse

This French classic, still enjoyed in bistros, smart restaurants and homes, relies on just three ingredients – the finest chocolate you can find, the freshest eggs and unsalted butter. Serve in pretty glasses or coffee cups, with crisp biscuits or Tiny Florentines (page 24).

85 g plain chocolate, finely chopped

2 tablespoons water, brandy or rum

10 g unsalted butter, at room temperature

3 large eggs, separated

*4 serving bowls, coffee cups or glasses*

Serves 4

Put the chocolate and water, brandy or rum into a heatproof bowl set over a saucepan of steaming but not boiling water and leave until just melted (do not let the base of the bowl touch the water). Remove the bowl from the heat and gently stir in the butter (it is vital to melt the chocolate gently without letting it get too hot, and to stir as little as possible). Leave for 1 minute, then gently stir in the egg yolks, one at a time.

Put the egg whites into a spotlessly clean, grease-free bowl and, using an electric whisk or mixer, whisk until stiff peaks form. Stir about one-quarter of the egg whites into the chocolate mixture to loosen it, then, using a large metal spoon, gently fold in the rest of the egg whites in 3 batches. Carefully spoon into serving bowls, cups or glasses, then chill for 2 hours before serving.

Best eaten within 12 hours. Not suitable for freezing.

### Variations

**Espresso Mousse**  Make the recipe above, replacing the water or brandy with 3 tablespoons of good quality espresso coffee, and whisking 3 tablespoons caster sugar into the stiff egg whites before adding them to the chocolate mixture.

**Cappuccino Mousse**  This is a creamy version of the espresso mousse above. Put 125 ml whipping cream into a mixing bowl and, using an electric whisk or mixer, whisk until soft peaks form. Fold half the cream into the mousse after the egg whites, then spoon into small coffee cups and chill for 2 hours. Just before serving, spoon the rest of the cream on top of the mousse, then sprinkle with cocoa or drinking chocolate.

Linzertorte is a classic dish dating back to the glory days of the Austrian Empire, and traditionally made from a nutty shortbread-like pastry and raspberry conserve. This recipe is not authentic, but fresh raspberries are the perfect contrast to the ultra-rich pastry. Serve with vanilla ice cream or whipped cream.

# fresh raspberry chocolate linzertorte

230 g hazelnuts

110 g unsalted butter, at room temperature

100 g icing sugar, sifted, plus extra for sprinkling

3 large egg yolks

200 g plain flour

½ teaspoon baking powder

2 teaspoons ground cinnamon

¼ teaspoon grated nutmeg

25 g cocoa powder

Raspberry filling

1½ tablespoons cornflour

3 tablespoons caster sugar, or to taste

600 g fresh raspberries

*a loose-based flan tin, 23 cm diameter, well buttered*

Serves 8

Put the hazelnuts into an ovenproof dish and toast in a preheated oven at 180°C (350°F) Gas 4 for about 15 minutes or until light golden brown. If the nuts still have their papery brown skin, put them in a clean dry tea towel, then gather up the ends and rub the nuts together to loosen the skins. Let cool, then transfer the skinned nuts to a food processor and grind to a fine powder.

Put the butter into a mixing bowl and, using a wooden spoon or electric mixer, beat until creamy. Add the icing sugar and beat, slowly at first, until light and fluffy. Beat in the egg yolks one at a time, beating well after each addition. Sift the flour, baking powder, cinnamon, nutmeg and cocoa onto the mixture and work in using a wooden spoon. Finally add the ground nuts and work in, using your hands to bring the pastry together.

Take three-quarters of the pastry and crumble it into the prepared tin. Using your fingers, press the pastry over the base and up the sides to cover the inside of the tin completely and form a layer about 1 cm thick. Chill for 15 minutes. Put the remaining pastry onto a well floured work surface and roll out, slightly thinner, to a rectangle about 23 x 14 cm. Cut into strips about 1 cm wide.

Sprinkle the cornflour and sugar over the raspberries and toss gently until almost mixed. Transfer the filling into the pastry case and spread it gently and evenly.

Arrange the lattice strips over the filling – if the pastry breaks, just push it back together again. Bake in the preheated oven at 180°C (350°F) Gas 4 for about 25–30 minutes, until the pastry is a slightly darker brown and just firm. Let cool, then remove from the pan and serve sprinkled with icing sugar.

Best eaten the same day. Not suitable for freezing.

Chocolate lovers in Italy are well served in Piedmont, in the far northwest. The capital city, Turin, is a veritable heaven-on-earth with irresistible pastry shops on every corner. One famous delight are the *gianduiotti*, chocolates made with dark chocolate and toasted hazelnuts. This torta also comes from Turin, but other recipes from the region are made with almonds or walnuts and flavoured with brandy, rum or grated orange zest. Use very fresh nuts for the best flavour.

# italian chocolate and hazelnut torta

100 g hazelnuts

100 g plain, crisp, butter biscuits, such as Petit Beurre, Abernethy or Osborne

100 g plain chocolate, finely chopped

1 large egg, at room temperature

1 large egg yolk, at room temperature

3 tablespoons caster sugar

75 g unsalted butter

cocoa powder, for sprinkling

whipped cream or ice cream, to serve

*a springform cake tin, 18 cm diameter, lightly buttered and base-lined*

*an ovenproof dish or baking sheet*

Serves 6–8

Put the hazelnuts into an ovenproof dish or onto a baking sheet and toast them in a preheated oven at 200°C (400°F) Gas 6 for 5 minutes or until lightly browned (watch them carefully as they will taste bitter if they become too dark). If the hazelnuts still have their papery brown skins, put them in a clean, dry tea towel, then gather up the ends and rub the nuts together to remove the skins. Leave the skinned nuts to cool, then chop very coarsely.

Put the biscuits into a food processor and work until coarse crumbs form. Alternatively, put the biscuits into a plastic bag and crush with a rolling pin.

Put the chocolate into a heatproof bowl set over a saucepan of steaming but not boiling water and melt gently (do not let the base of the bowl touch the water).

Meanwhile, put the whole egg, egg yolk and sugar into a mixing bowl and, using an electric mixer, electric hand whisk or rotary whisk, whisk vigorously until the mixture is very pale, thick and mousse-like – when the whisk is lifted, a thick ribbon-like trail slowly falls back into the bowl. Heat the butter in a small, heavy-based saucepan until just bubbling. Pour the hot butter onto the mixture in a thin steady stream while still whisking at top speed (this is not so easy with a rotary whisk), then whisk in the melted chocolate. Using a large metal spoon, gently fold in the chopped nuts and crushed biscuits. When thoroughly mixed, pour the mixture into the prepared tin, spreading it gently and evenly. Cover the top of the tin with clingfilm, then chill for at least 3 hours or overnight, until firm.

To serve, unclip the tin and remove the torta. Set on a serving plate, sprinkle with cocoa and serve, well chilled, with whipped cream or ice cream.

Best eaten within 5 days. Do not freeze.

A delicious finale for a lovely summertime dinner, serve this
very light cake with piles of berries and whipped cream.

# italian chocolate amaretto torta

110 g plain chocolate, chopped

2 tablespoons Amaretto liqueur

110 g unsalted butter,
at room temperature

110 g caster sugar, plus 1 tablespoon

3 large eggs, separated

60 g amaretti biscuits, crushed

60 g plain flour, sifted

**To serve**

whipped cream

blueberries, raspberries or baked apricots

*a loose-based sandwich tin,
20 cm diameter, buttered,
base-lined, then floured*

**Serves 8**

Put the chocolate and Amaretto into a heatproof bowl set over a saucepan of steaming but not boiling water and leave until melted (do not let the base of the bowl touch the water). Remove the bowl from the heat, stir gently and let cool.

Put the butter and the 110 g caster sugar into a mixing bowl and, using a wooden spoon or electric mixer, beat until very light and fluffy. Beat in the egg yolks one at a time, then stir in the cooled chocolate. When thoroughly blended, use a large metal spoon to fold in the crushed biscuits and flour.

Put the egg whites into a spotlessly clean, grease-free bowl and, using an electric whisk or mixer, whisk until stiff peaks form. Whisk in the remaining 1 tablespoon sugar to make a stiff, glossy meringue, then fold into the cake mixture in 3 batches.

Transfer the mixture to the prepared tin and bake in a preheated oven at 180°C (350°F) Gas 4 for 30–35 minutes until just firm to the touch. Let cool in the tin for 10 minutes. Remove from the tin and transfer to a wire rack to cool completely.

Sprinkle with icing sugar and serve slightly warm or at room temperature with whipped cream and fresh berries. Alternatively, sprinkle halved apricots with sugar, Amaretto and crushed amaretti, bake until soft, then serve with the torta.

Best eaten within 3 days. Not suitable for freezing.

# black cherry frangipane tart

Almonds, cherries and chocolate work so well together – the flavours and textures bring out the best in each other. Serve with vanilla ice cream or crème fraîche.

175 g plain flour

a pinch of salt

1 tablespoon caster sugar

115 g unsalted butter, chilled and cut into small pieces

vanilla ice cream or crème fraîche, to serve

Almond filling

125 g unsalted butter, at room temperature

125 g caster sugar

2 large eggs, beaten

2 teaspoons kirsch or 1 teaspoon almond essence

125 g ground almonds

25 g plain flour

75 g plain chocolate, finely chopped, plus 40 g extra, melted, to finish

400 g black or red cherries, pitted

*a loose-based flan tin, 24 cm diameter, buttered*

*baking paper and baking beans or dried beans*

Serves 6–8

1 To make the pastry in a food processor, put the flour, salt, sugar and butter into the machine and process until the mixture resembles fine crumbs. With the machine running, add 3 tablespoons iced water through the feed tube, then process until the pastry comes together. If there are dry crumbs, add a little more water, 1 tablespoon at a time, until you have a slightly firm pastry.

**Alternatively**, to make the pastry by hand, sift the flour, salt and sugar into a mixing bowl. Add the pieces of butter and, using the tips of your fingers, rub into the flour. When the mixture resembles breadcrumbs, use a round-bladed knife to stir in 3 tablespoons iced water to make a firm pastry. Wrap and chill for 15 minutes.

2 Put the pastry onto a lightly floured work surface and, using a rolling pin, roll out the pastry to a large circle, about 28 cm diameter.

3 Carefully lift the pastry with the rolling pin and use it to line the prepared flan tin.

**4** Press the pastry into the corners and fluting of the tin. Roll the pin over the top to cut off the excess pastry.

**5** Prick the base all over with a fork, then chill for 15 minutes.

**6** Line the pastry case with a piece of baking parchment a little larger than the circle of pastry. Fill with baking beans or dried beans to hold the paper down, then bake in a preheated oven at 190°C (375°F) Gas 5 for 10 minutes. This is called 'baking blind'.

**7** Remove the paper and beans and bake for a further 5 minutes. Remove from the oven and let cool.

**8** To make the filling, put the butter and sugar into a mixing bowl and, using a wooden spoon or electric mixer, beat until light and fluffy.

**9** Gradually beat in the eggs and kirsch.

**10** Using a large metal spoon, fold in the ground almonds and flour.

**11** Scatter the chopped chocolate over the base of the pastry case. Top with an even layer of cherries.

**12** Spoon the almond mixture on top and spread evenly. Bake in a preheated oven at 190°C (375°F) Gas 5 for about 30 minutes until golden brown and firm to the touch. Remove from the oven, let cool on a wire rack, then carefully remove from the flan tin.

**13** To finish, drizzle the melted chocolate over the top with a fork, then leave to set. Serve at room temperature with vanilla ice cream or crème fraîche.

Best eaten within 3 days. Not suitable for freezing.

This slightly unusual cheesecake from Italy – very light in texture yet full of flavour – can be eaten warm or at room temperature. Mascarpone is an Italian cheese made from thick, fresh cream, which has not been left to ripen or ferment – this gives it a slightly sweet taste and an extremely rich texture.

# warm chocolate mascarpone cheesecake

### Biscuit base

225 g digestive or wheaten biscuits

60 g unsalted butter

60 g plain chocolate, finely chopped

### Chocolate filling

2 large eggs, separated

85 g caster sugar

230 g mascarpone cheese

150 ml double cream, lightly whipped

50 g plain chocolate, very finely chopped

4 tablespoons cocoa powder, sifted

45 g ground almonds

1–2 tablespoons Amaretto liqueur or brandy

icing sugar, for sprinkling

ice cream or thick cream, to serve

*a springform cake tin, 23 cm diameter, well buttered*

### Serves 8

To make the base, put the biscuits into a food processor and pulse until fine crumbs form. Alternatively, put the biscuits into a plastic bag and crush with a rolling pin. Transfer the crumbs into a mixing bowl. Put the butter and chocolate into a heatproof bowl set over a saucepan of steaming but not boiling water and melt gently (do not let the base of the bowl touch the water). Remove from the heat, stir gently, then stir into the biscuit crumbs. When well mixed, transfer the mixture to the prepared tin and, using the back of a spoon, press onto the base and about halfway up the sides of the tin. Chill while making the filling.

To make the filling, put the egg yolks and sugar into a large mixing bowl and, using an electric whisk or mixer, whisk until very thick and mousse-like – when the whisk is lifted, a wide ribbon-like trail slowly falls back into the bowl. Put the mascarpone into a separate bowl, beat until smooth, then gently fold in the whipped cream.

Gently stir the mascarpone mixture into the egg yolks, then add the chopped chocolate, cocoa, ground almonds and liqueur and mix gently.

Put the egg whites into a spotlessly clean, grease-free bowl and, using an electric whisk or mixer, whisk until stiff peaks form. Using a large metal spoon, fold the egg whites into the mixture in 3 batches.

Pour the filling into the biscuit case and bake in a preheated oven at 170°C (325°F) Gas 3 for about 1 hour or until set and beginning to colour. Remove from the oven and let cool for about 20 minutes, then carefully unclip and remove the tin. Sprinkle with icing sugar and serve warm or at room temperature with ice cream or thick cream.

This famous pie comes from the South of the USA – it is supposed to look like the thick, dark, muddy waters of the Mississippi delta. It is very easy to make and is perfect to share with family and friends.

# mississippi mud pie

**Biscuit base**

225 g digestive or wheaten biscuits

60 g unsalted butter

60 g plain chocolate, finely chopped

**Chocolate filling**

180 g plain chocolate, chopped

180 g unsalted butter, cut into small pieces

4 large eggs, beaten

90 g light muscovado sugar

90 g dark muscovado sugar

180 ml double cream

**Chocolate cream**

140 ml double cream, well chilled

3 tablespoons cocoa powder

40 g icing sugar

*a springform cake tin, 23 cm diameter, well buttered*

Serves 8

To make the base, put the biscuits into a food processor and process until fine crumbs form. Alternatively, put the biscuits into a plastic bag and crush with a rolling pin. Transfer the crumbs into a mixing bowl.

Put the butter and chocolate into a heatproof bowl set over a saucepan of steaming but not boiling water and melt gently (do not let the base of the bowl touch the water). Remove from the heat, stir gently, then stir into the biscuit crumbs. When well mixed, transfer the mixture to the prepared tin and, using the back of a spoon, press onto the base and about halfway up the sides of the tin. Chill while making the filling.

To make the filling, put the chocolate and butter into a heatproof bowl set over a saucepan of steaming but not boiling water and melt gently (do not let the base of the bowl touch the water). Remove from the heat, stir gently, then let cool.

Put the eggs and sugar into a large mixing bowl and, using an electric whisk or mixer, whisk until thick and foamy. Whisk in the cream followed by the melted chocolate. Pour the mixture into the biscuit case and bake in a preheated oven at 180°C (350°F) Gas 4 for about 45 minutes until just firm. Let cool for a few minutes, then remove from the tin.

To make the chocolate cream, put the cream into a mixing bowl, then sift the cocoa and icing sugar on top and stir gently with a wooden spoon until blended. Cover and chill for 2 hours.

Serve the pie at room temperature with the chocolate cream. The pie can be made up to 2 days in advance and kept well covered in the refrigerator. Remove from the refrigerator 30 minutes before serving.

# sticky chocolate pecan pie

Incredibly rich and gooey, this is a real treat. The short, crumbly pastry is simple to make in a food processor, and the filling has a wonderfully fudgy taste and texture. Use a freshly opened packet of pecans for best results.

180 g plain flour, plus extra for dusting

a pinch of salt

1 tablespoon caster sugar

115 g unsalted butter, chilled and cut into small pieces

1 large egg yolk mixed with 1 tablespoon cold water

vanilla ice cream or whipped cream, to serve

### Chocolate filling

45 g unsalted butter, softened

125 g light muscovado sugar

150 ml golden syrup

3 large eggs, beaten

1 teaspoon vanilla essence

100 g plain chocolate, melted

100 g pecan nuts

*a loose-based flan tin, 23 cm diameter, well buttered*

*baking parchment and baking beans or dried beans*

Serves 8

To make the pastry in a food processor, put the flour, salt, sugar and butter into the bowl and process until the mixture resembles fine crumbs. With the machine running, add the egg yolk and water through the feed tube. Run the machine until the pastry comes together. If there are dry crumbs, add a teaspoon or so more water.

If making the pastry by hand, sift the flour, salt and sugar into a large mixing bowl. Add the butter and rub in using the tips of your fingers. When the mixture resembles crumbs, stir in the yolk mixture with a round-bladed knife to make a firm pastry. Wrap and chill for 15 minutes until firm.

Put the pastry onto a floured work surface and, using a rolling pin, roll out to a large circle about 6 cm larger than the flan tin, then use to line the tin. Prick the base of the pastry case with a fork, then chill for 15 minutes.

Line the pastry case with a sheet of non-stick baking parchment, then fill with baking beans or dried beans. Bake 'blind' in a preheated oven at 180°C (350°F) Gas 4 for about 12 minutes, then carefully remove the paper and beans. Bake for a further 10 minutes until lightly golden and just firm. Remove from the oven and let cool while making the filling.

Put the butter, sugar and golden syrup into a mixing bowl and, using a wooden spoon or electric mixer, beat until smooth. Gradually beat in the eggs and then the vanilla essence. Stir in the melted chocolate followed by the pecan nuts.

Pour the mixture into the prepared pastry case and bake in a preheated oven at 180°C (350°F) Gas 4 for 35 minutes until just firm to the touch. Remove from the oven and let cool – the filling will sink slightly. Serve warm or at room temperature with vanilla ice cream or whipped cream.

Best eaten within 4 days.

# chocolate fondue

100 g plain chocolate, chopped

100 g white chocolate, chopped

100 g milk chocolate, chopped

9 tablespoons double cream

1 tablespoon Bacardi rum
or Grand Marnier (optional)

To serve

1 small pineapple

2 medium bananas

125 g strawberries

125 g cherries

2 medium pears

*a fondue set, small saucepans
or heatproof bowls*

Serves 4–6

This recipe comes from Michael Levy of Le Chocolatier in Great Barrow, near Chester – one of the world's most renowned factories, specializing in 'couture' chocolate. (see Mail Order Sources, page 126). It is a very simple idea for creating a marvellous special occasion pudding. Buy the chocolate you like to eat (there is a huge variety of brands and types available). Use small saucepans or pretty heatproof bowls set on the table over a warming tray or three candle-warmers – and have lots of fun.

Put each type of chocolate into small, heatproof bowls set over small saucepans of steaming but not boiling water and melt gently (do not let the base of the bowls touch the water).

Put the cream into a separate saucepan, bring to the boil, then add 3 tablespoons to each saucepan or bowl of melted chocolate and mix gently. If using Bacardi or Grand Marnier, add it to the white chocolate mixture.

Set the saucepans or bowls over the lowest possible heat on a warming tray in the centre of the table, surrounded by the fruit. Cut the fruit at the table and immediately dip into the melted chocolate fondues and eat.

# chocolate sauces

## rich dark chocolate sauce

For a creamy sauce, use single cream instead of
the water or, for a flavoured sauce replace some
of the water with a tablespoon or so of brandy,
rum or coffee liqueur.

100 g plain chocolate, finely chopped
60 g unsalted butter, cut into small pieces

Serves 4–6

Put the chopped chocolate, butter and 100 ml water into a
heatproof bowl set over a saucepan of steaming but not boiling
water (do not let the base of the bowl touch the water). Stir
frequently until melted and very smooth.

Remove from the heat and stir well until glossy and slightly
thickened. As the sauce cools, it will become even thicker.
Serve warm.

## creamy chocolate sauce

A very quick, rich sauce for ice cream, profiteroles
and steamed puddings. Just before serving it can
be flavoured with rum, brandy or coffee liqueur. For
a slightly thinner, less rich sauce, use single cream,
or cream mixed half and half with milk or coffee.

125 ml double cream
85 g plain chocolate, finely chopped
½ teaspoon vanilla essence

Serves 4–6

Put the cream into a small, heavy-based saucepan and heat
gently, stirring frequently. When the cream comes to the boil,
remove from the heat. Let cool for 1 minute, then stir in the
chopped chocolate. Stir gently until the sauce is smooth. Stir
in the vanilla essence and serve immediately.

## chocolate custard sauce

The classic sauce for steamed puddings.

450 ml full-cream milk

3 tablespoons cocoa powder

60 g caster sugar

1 tablespoon cornflour

2 egg yolks

Serves 4–6

Put all but 2 tablespoons of the milk into a large, heavy-based saucepan and heat until almost boiling. Sift the cocoa, sugar and cornflour into a heatproof bowl, stir in the egg yolks and the 2 tablespoons cold milk to form a thick paste, then stir in the hot milk. Strain the mixture back into the saucepan and stir constantly over low heat until the mixture thickens — do not let the mixture boil or it will curdle.

Remove from the heat and use immediately, or keep it warm until ready to serve.

## white chocolate sauce

The flavour depends on the quality of the chocolate, so use the best you can lay your hands on rather than children's bars.

200 g good quality white chocolate, finely chopped

200 ml double cream

80 ml milk

Serves 4–6

Put the chocolate into a heatproof bowl set over a saucepan of steaming but not boiling water and melt gently (do not let the base of the bowl touch the water). Remove from the heat and stir gently until smooth.

Put the cream and milk into a small, heavy-based saucepan and heat until scalding hot, but not quite boiling. Remove from the heat. Pour the mixture onto the chocolate in a thin stream, whisking constantly, to make a smooth sauce. Pour into a warmed jug and serve immediately.

# ice cream

The ultimate luxury on a hot day has to be freshly churned ice cream with crunchy wafers or crisp cones. A small, easy-to-use ice cream maker will pay for itself in a season. If you have to make these recipes by hand, just part-freeze the mixture, then beat with a fork. Repeat several times, then let freeze completely.

# deluxe chocolate ice cream

A truly rich and luxurious recipe – to make it even richer, stir in some crushed praline (page 30) at the same time as the cream.

200 g plain chocolate, finely chopped

300 ml milk

1 large vanilla pod, split lengthways

3 large egg yolks

75 g caster sugar

200 ml double cream, well chilled

*an ice cream maker or freezer-proof container*

Serves 4–6

Put the chocolate into a large bowl. Pour the milk into a medium, heavy-based saucepan and add the vanilla pod. Heat slowly over low heat, stirring frequently, until the milk is fairly hot – around 60°C (140°F) – then remove from the heat, cover and leave to infuse for 15–20 minutes.

Put the egg yolks and sugar into a bowl and mix well. Add the warm milk and mix thoroughly. Pour the mixture back into the saucepan and stir over low heat until thick enough to coat the back of a wooden spoon – do not let the mixture boil or it will curdle.

Remove the saucepan from the heat and discard the vanilla pod. Pour the custard onto the chopped chocolate and stir until smooth. Let cool, then cover and chill thoroughly. Put a bowl and whisk into the refrigerator to chill. When chilled, pour the cream into the cold bowl and, using the whisk, whip until soft peaks form. Stir in the chocolate custard.

Pour the mixture into an ice cream maker and churn until frozen. Eat immediately or store in the freezer. Alternatively, put the mixture into a freezer-proof container and freeze, stirring occasionally.

# white chocolate ice cream

The taste of this ice cream depends entirely on the quality of the white chocolate. My favourite brand is Green & Black Organic, flavoured with vanilla, which is not too cloyingly sweet.

150 g white chocolate, finely chopped

225 ml milk

225 ml double cream

1 vanilla pod, split lengthways

4 large egg yolks

60 g caster sugar

*an ice cream maker or freezer-proof container*

Serves 4–6

Put the chocolate into a large bowl. Pour the milk and cream into a medium, heavy-based saucepan, add the vanilla pod and stir gently over low heat until the milk is fairly hot – around 60°C (140°F) – then remove from the heat, cover and leave to infuse for 15–20 minutes.

Put the egg yolks and sugar into a bowl and mix well. Add the hot milk and stir well. Pour the mixture back into the saucepan and stir over low heat until thick enough to coat the back of a wooden spoon – don't let the mixture boil or it will curdle.

Remove the saucepan from the heat, discard the vanilla pod, then let cool for 2 minutes. Pour the custard onto the chopped chocolate and stir until smooth. Let cool, then cover and chill thoroughly.

Pour the mixture into an ice cream maker and churn until frozen. Eat immediately or store in the freezer. Alternatively, put the mixture into a freezer-proof container and freeze, stirring occasionally.

# pistachio and chocolate ice cream

Nobody makes pistachio ice cream like the Italians, but this home-style version is fairly authentic. Most supermarkets sell shelled unsalted pistachios – the roasted and salted snack kind aren't suitable for this recipe. Fresh nuts taste best, so use a fresh pack.

100 g shelled unsalted pistachios
250 ml double cream, well chilled
300 ml milk
4 large egg yolks
100 g caster sugar
85 g plain chocolate, finely chopped

*an ice cream maker or freezer-proof container*

Serves 4–6

Put the pistachios and 3 tablespoons of the cream into a food processor or blender and process to a fine paste, scraping down the sides from time to time. Transfer the paste to a medium, heavy-based saucepan and stir in the milk. Heat gently until almost boiling, stirring frequently, then remove from the heat, cover and leave to infuse for 15–20 minutes.

Put the egg yolks and sugar into a bowl and mix well. Pour in the pistachio milk and stir well. Pour the mixture back into the saucepan. Stir gently over low heat until the mixture thickens – do not let it boil or it will curdle. Remove from the heat, pour into a clean jug or bowl, let cool, then chill thoroughly. Put a bowl and whisk into the refrigerator to chill.

When ready to churn, put the rest of the cream into the chilled bowl and, using the whisk, whip until soft peaks form, then stir in the pistachio mixture and the chopped chocolate. Pour into an ice cream maker and churn until frozen. Eat immediately or store in the freezer. Alternatively, put the mixture into a freezer-proof container and freeze, stirring occasionally.

# rich mocha ice cream

On a hot day, this is a great mid-morning reviver. I've tried this recipe made with all types of coffee – espresso, instant, concentrate, freshly brewed, ground coffee, but beans work best.

350 ml milk
3 tablespoons coffee beans
4 large egg yolks
80 g caster sugar
250 ml double cream, well chilled
100 g plain chocolate, chopped

*an ice cream maker or freezer-proof container*

Serves 4–6

Put the milk into a medium, heavy-based saucepan. Put the coffee beans into an electric coffee grinder and crack roughly. Alternatively, put them in a dry tea towel and crush with a heavy pan. Add to the saucepan and heat until the milk almost boils. Remove from the heat, cover and leave to infuse for 15–20 minutes.

Put the egg yolks and sugar into a bowl and mix well. Strain the warm milk onto the mixture, stir well, then pour back into the saucepan. Stir over low heat until thick enough to coat the back of a wooden spoon – do not let the mixture boil or it will curdle. Remove from the heat, strain into a bowl, let cool, then chill. Put a bowl and whisk into the refrigerator to chill.

When ready to churn, put the cream into the chilled bowl and, using the whisk, whip until soft peaks form. Carefully stir into the coffee custard. Pour into an ice cream maker and churn until very thick. Add the chopped chocolate and churn until frozen. Eat immediately or store in the freezer. Alternatively, put the mixture into a freezer-proof container and freeze, stirring frequently, until very thick, then stir in the chocolate and freeze until firm.

# maple pecan ice cream

An ice cream flavoured with maple syrup instead of sugar is great with Brownies (page 59)!

100 g pecan nuts

6 tablespoons maple syrup

300 ml milk

3 large egg yolks

150 g plain chocolate, finely chopped

200 ml double cream, well chilled

*a baking dish, well-oiled*

*an ice cream maker or freezer-proof container*

Serves 4–6

Put the pecans (they can be whole or in large pieces) into the well-oiled baking dish, then add 1 tablespoon of the maple syrup and mix until the nuts are thoroughly coated. Toast in a preheated oven at 180°C (350°F) Gas 4 for 10 minutes, then remove and let cool in the dish.

Put the milk into a heavy-based saucepan and heat gently. Put the egg yolks into a bowl, then stir in the remaining syrup. Pour in the warm milk and stir well. Pour the mixture back into the saucepan and stir gently over low heat until thick enough to coat the back of a wooden spoon – do not let the mixture boil or it will curdle. Remove the saucepan from the heat.

Put the chocolate into a large bowl and gently stir in the warm custard until smooth. Let cool, then cover and chill thoroughly. Put a bowl and whisk into the refrigerator to chill. When chilled, put the cream into the cold bowl and, using the whisk, whip the cream until soft peaks form. Stir in the cold custard. Pour into an ice cream maker and churn until thick. Add the toasted nuts and churn again until frozen. Eat immediately or store in the freezer. Alternatively, put the mixture into a freezer–proof container and freeze, stirring occasionally, until almost frozen, then stir in the nuts and freeze until firm.

# intensely chocolate sorbet

A delicious recipe with just three ingredients – will your guests guess the spicy secret?

150 g plain chocolate, very finely chopped

125 g caster sugar

1 small dried red chilli

*an ice cream maker or freezer-proof container*

Serves 4

Put the chopped chocolate into a large heatproof bowl. Put the sugar and 230 ml water into a medium, heavy-based saucepan and heat very gently until the sugar has completely melted. Bring the mixture to the boil and boil for 2 minutes until slightly syrupy. Add the dried chilli, then remove the saucepan from the heat, cover and leave to infuse for 15 minutes.

If necessary, reheat the syrup until just warmer than your finger can stand, then strain the syrup onto the chocolate and stir gently until the mixture is smooth. Leave until cold, then pour into an ice cream maker and churn until frozen. Eat immediately or store in the freezer. Alternatively, put the mixture into a freezer-proof container and freeze, stirring or whisking frequently.

**Variations** If the Aztec flavouring doesn't appeal (the flavour is subtle and mysterious) replace the chilli with a small bunch of fresh mint leaves. Slightly bruise the leaves with a rolling pin, then add to the hot syrup and leave to infuse as in the main recipe. Alternatively, use a vanilla pod split lengthways, a broken up cinnamon stick, a large star anise or even 1 tablespoon of your favourite coffee beans.

# cones and wafers

## chocolate ice cream wafers

175 g plain flour

a pinch of salt

½ teaspoon baking powder

25 g cocoa powder

110 g caster sugar

125 g unsalted butter, cut into small pieces

1 teaspoon vanilla essence

*several baking sheets, lined with non-stick baking parchment*

Makes 14–16

Sift the flour, salt, baking powder, cocoa and sugar into a food processor. Add the butter and vanilla and process until the dough comes together into a ball. Shape into a brick, about 10 x 7 x 5 cm. Wrap in greaseproof paper and chill until firm. Using a sharp knife, cut the dough into wafer-thin slices. Set apart on the baking sheets and bake in a preheated oven at 200°C (400°F) Gas 6 for about 5–7 minutes until just firm and the edges are starting to colour. Let cool for 2 minutes until firm enough to transfer to a wire rack.

Best eaten within 5 days. The dough can be kept in the refrigerator for up to 1 week or frozen for up to 1 month.

## chocolate ice cream cones

Simple, really – and the perfect way to provide an extra dose of chocolate for the truly committed chocolate lover.

100 g plain chocolate

8 ice cream cones

*a pastry brush*

*several baking sheets, lined with non-stick baking parchment*

Makes 8

Put the chocolate into a heatproof bowl set over a saucepan of steaming but not boiling water and melt gently (do not let the base of the bowl touch the water). Using a pastry brush, brush the inside of the cones with the melted chocolate. Arrange on the baking sheets and let set in a cool place (or the refrigerator in very hot weather).

## chocolate baskets

Whisked egg whites are the basis for these crisp tuile biscuits. The mixture must be spread thinly, baked until light brown, then quickly draped over an orange to give a basket shape. The biscuits can also be rolled up. Don't worry if the first couple you make are not perfect – you'll soon get the hang of it.

2 large egg whites

110 g caster sugar

55 g plain flour

55 g unsalted butter, melted and cooled

30 g plain chocolate, very finely chopped

grated zest of 1 unwaxed orange

*several baking sheets, lined with non-stick baking parchment*

Makes about 16

Put the egg whites into a spotlessly clean, grease-free bowl and, using an electric or rotary whisk or mixer, whisk until stiff peaks form. Whisk in the sugar. Sift the flour onto the whites, gently fold it in using a large metal spoon, then fold in the cooled melted butter, chocolate and orange zest.

Put a scant tablespoon of the mixture onto a prepared baking sheet and spread thinly with the back of a spoon to make a 12 cm disc. Make another disc in the same way, then bake in a preheated oven at 180°C (350°F) Gas 4 for 7–10 minutes until lightly browned. Continue making and baking 2 discs at a time.

Using a palette knife, carefully lift each tuile off the tray and, while still hot, drape over an orange so it cools and sets in a basket shape. The hot tuiles can also be rolled around the handle of a wooden spoon to make thin, crisp, rolled-up biscuits. If the tuiles become too cool to shape, return them to the oven for 1 minute to soften. Store in an airtight container.

Best eaten within 24 hours.

# drinks

Chocolate was originally consumed as a frothy, intensely flavoured, high-status drink for the well-off. More recently, chocolate drinks were thought of as a comforting bedtime treat—but now it's time for them to come in from the cold!

# the finest hot chocolate

85 g plain chocolate, broken into pieces

1 tablespoon caster sugar, or to taste

1 vanilla pod, split lengthways

300 ml milk

100 ml whipping cream, whipped

freshly grated chocolate or cocoa powder, for sprinkling

2 mugs, warmed

Serves 2

The ultimate hot drink – the best quality chocolate, a hint of vanilla, lots of frothy milk topped with whipped cream and grated chocolate. This is what chocolate lovers have been waiting for. Make sure the mugs or cups are warmed beforehand and, for a real treat, serve with Giant Double Chocolate Nut Cookies (page 67).

Put the chocolate pieces, sugar, vanilla pod and milk into a small, heavy-based saucepan. Heat gently, stirring, until the chocolate has melted, then bring to the boil, whisking constantly with a balloon whisk, until very smooth and frothy. Remove the vanilla pod.

Pour into warmed mugs, top with whipped cream and a sprinkling of freshly grated chocolate or cocoa and serve immediately.

# monsieur st disdiers' chocolate

50 g plain chocolate, finely chopped

30 g caster sugar, or to taste

2 large pinches of ground cinnamon

½ vanilla pod, split lengthways

*4 cups, warmed*

Serves 4

This French recipe was first recorded in 1692 and soon became a court favourite in England. I tasted it during an Easter chocolate celebration at Hampton Court Palace, where historians were on hand to describe how chocolate was prepared for William III. Monsieur St Disdiers was the first Royal Chocolate Maker – the King enjoyed chocolate so much he installed a special chocolate kitchen in the royal apartments in 1699. Making the chocolate drink for the King was a job for an expert, and good chocolate makers were highly prized. The froth was very important – some cooks would add egg white to increase the volume of the froth. It is incredibly rich, so serve it in small quantities.

Put 300 ml water into a heavy-based saucepan, bring to the boil, then remove from the heat and add the chocolate, sugar and cinnamon. Using the tip of a small knife, scrape the seeds from the vanilla pod into the saucepan.

Using a balloon whisk, whisk constantly for a few minutes, taking care not to splash the boiling liquid. When a good amount of froth has been created, pour the chocolate into warmed cups, then spoon the froth on top and serve.

# john nott's wine chocolate

425 ml port

50 g plain chocolate, grated

75 g caster sugar, or to taste

1 teaspoon cornflour

*4 cups or mugs, warmed*

Serves 4

At Syon House in Isleworth, the country house of the Dukes of Northumberland, the food historian Peter Brears prepared this drink created by the pastry cook John Nott at Syon in 1726. It sounds odd, but tastes delicious.

Put all the ingredients into a heavy saucepan and whisk well. Bring to the boil, whisking constantly, then serve.

# hot spanish

Dip tall cinnamon sticks into melted chocolate, leave to set, then use to stir this special drink.

50 g plain chocolate, broken into pieces

225 ml milk

1 tablespoon caster sugar

1 cinnamon stick

300 ml hot, strong black coffee

2 tablespoons brandy (optional)

2 curls of fresh orange peel

*2 tall heatproof glasses, warmed*

## Serves 2

Put the chocolate, milk, sugar and cinnamon into a small, heavy-based saucepan and heat gently, stirring constantly, until melted and smooth. Bring the mixture to the boil, whisking constantly with a balloon whisk, then remove from the heat and whisk in the coffee and brandy, if using. Remove the cinnamon stick. Put the curls of orange peel into tall, warmed, heatproof glasses, pour over the hot mixture and serve.

# hot mocha

This is a truly classic coffee-chocolate combination. For best results, use freshly brewed coffee.

100 g plain chocolate, broken into pieces

1 tablespoon caster sugar, or to taste

300 ml milk

450 ml hot, strong black coffee

100 ml whipping cream, whipped

*4 large mugs, warmed*

## Serves 4

Put the chocolate, sugar and milk into a small, heavy-based saucepan and stir over low heat until melted and smooth. Bring to the boil, whisking constantly with a balloon whisk, then remove from the heat and whisk in the hot coffee. Pour into warmed mugs, top with whipped cream and serve immediately.

### Variation

**Iced Mocha**  Follow the recipe for Hot Mocha, but omit the cream. Make up the mixture of chocolate, sugar, milk and coffee as given, then let cool and chill. Put the mixture into a blender, add 3 scoops (about 85 g) vanilla ice cream (optional) and blend briefly. Fill tall, chilled glasses with ice cubes, then pour over the mocha drink and serve immediately.

# mail order sources and websites

**THE CHOCOLATE SOCIETY**

**The Chocolate Society**
Clay Pit Lane
Roecliffe
Boroughbridge
North Yorkshire YO51 9LS
Tel: 01423 322230
Email: info@chocolate.co.uk
www.chocolate.co.uk
**(London Shop)**
36 Elizabeth Street
London SW1W 9NZ
Tel 020 7259 9222
*Twice-yearly newsletter with
everything you need to know about
the world of chocolate, plus an
extensive range of high quality
handmade goodies and Valrhona
products available from the shop
and by mail order.*

**CHOCOLATE SHOPS**

**L'Artisan du Chocolat**
89 Lower Sloane Street
London SW1 W8DA
Tel: 020 7824 8365
Email: atelierduchocolat@aol.com
*Shop selling unusual and couture
chocolates handmade by Gerard
Coleman, truffles, bars and
gâteaux, plus ready chopped
Valrhona chocolate for melting and
cooking. Mail order available.*

**Rococo**
321 King's Road
London SW3 5EP
Tel: 020 7352 5857
Email:
james@rococochocolates.com
www.rococochocolates.com
*Chantal Coady makes organic
chocolates, and specializes in
artisan bars with surprising
ingredients, plus Valrhona. Available
from the shop and by mail order.*

**Theobroma Cacao**
43 Turnham Green Terrace
London W4 1RG
Tel: 020 8996 0431
*Wonderful handmade chocolates
and gâteaux (especially chocolate
wedding cakes) plus an extensive
range of high quality chocolate
products for the home baker.*

**Le Chocolatier**
8 Barrowmore Estate
Great Barrow
Nr Chester CH3 7JA
Tel: 01829 741010
Email: michael@cocoasolid.com
www.cocoasolid.com
*Michael Levy creates superb
handmade chocolates, and sells
the highest quality chocolate for the
home baker and for melting, plus
moulds and equipment, all available
by mail order only. He also gives
tutored tastings, talks and
demonstrations.*

**Valvona and Crolla**
19 Elm Row
Edinburgh EH7 4AA
Tel: 0131 556 6066
Fax: 0131 556 1688
www.valvonacrolla.co.uk
*Excellent shop with good range of
chocolate including Valrhona.
Phone for mail-order details.*

**Valrhona Factory Shop**
14 Avenue President Roosevelt
26601Tain l'Hermitage, France
Tel: 0033 475 07 90 090
Email: info@valrhona.fr
www.valrhona.com
*This Rhône Valley factory produces
Valrhona chocolate, known to
cooks everywhere as one of the
best. Website includes recipes and
news, plus links to retailers around
the world.*

**Bernachon**
42 Cours Franklin Roosevelt
69006 Lyon, France
Tel: 0033 78.24.37.98
*The Bernachons make chocolate
from scratch – buying the beans,
roasting, grinding, mixing and
conching – the full works to make
their unique and exceptional
chocolate. The chocolate is used
for handmade truffles, chocolates
and gâteaux. Their shop is a
magnificent temple to their craft,
and their chocolates are only
available there, at Paul Bocuse's
restaurant nearby or by
mail order.*

**Bettys of Harrogate**
1 Parliament Street
Harrogate, HG1 2QU
Tel: 01423 877 300
**(Other tearooms)**
6–8 St Helen's Square, York
46 Stonegate, York
32 The Grove, Ilkley
188 High Street, Northallerton
*Tearooms and shops selling
handmade cakes, pastries and
chocolates. The original and most
famous is on the site of the
Edwardian Imperial Tearooms
in Harrogate.*
**Bettys by Post**
Tel: 01423 814008
www.bettysbypost.com
*Mail order and website selling
handmade cakes, pastries and
chocolates.*
**Bettys Cookery School**
Hookstone Park
Hookstone Chase
Harrogate
North Yorkshire HG2 7LD
Tel: 01423 814016
*If you want to learn from a master
chocolatier, Bettys new purpose-
built cookery school at Starbeck,
Harrogate is the place. Their
handmade chocolates are also
available by mail order.*

**EQUIPMENT AND UTENSILS**

**Lakeland Limited**
Alexandra Buildings
Windermere
Cumbria LA23 1BQ
Tel: 015394 88100
Fax: 015394 88300
www.lakelandlimited.com
*Huge range of high quality
bakeware and cookery equipment
available by mail order, online and
from their shops. Some hard-to-
find ingredients also available.
Fast and friendly service. Phone
for a catalogue.*

**Silverwood Limited**
Ledsam Street Works
Birmingham B16 8DN
Tel: 0121 454 3571/2
Fax: 0121 454 6749
Email:
Sales@AlanSilverwood.co.uk
*Professional quality bread and cake
tins and trays; bakeware which
should last a lifetime. Aga range
too. Stocked by Lakeland, John
Lewis stores, major department
stores and cook shops. For local
stockists write or phone for details.*

**Divertimenti**
139–141 Fulham Road
London SW3 6SD
Tel: 020 7581 8065
Fax: 020 7823 9429
33–34 Marylebone High Street
London W1U 4PT
Tel: 020 7935 0689
www.divertimenti.co.uk
*Two shops in London plus mail
order catalogue for a wide range
of equipmen. Knife sharpening
and copper retinning service.
On-line cooks' chatroom
'The Kitchen Table'.*

**David Mellor**
4 Sloane Square
London SW1 8EE
Tel: 020 7730 4259
www.davidmellordesign.co.uk
*Well-stocked shop plus mail
order catalogue.*

# index